D0746855

CREATIVE

PROBLEM-SOLVING

IN

ETHICS

CREATIVE

PROBLEM-SOLVING

IN

ETHICS

Anthony Weston

New York   Oxford
OXFORD UNIVERSITY PRESS
2007

Oxford University Press, Inc., publishes works that further Oxford
University's objective of excellence in research, scholarship, and education.

Oxford   New York
Auckland   Cape Town   Dar es Salaam   Hong Kong   Karachi
Kuala Lumpur   Madrid   Melbourne   Mexico City   Nairobi
New Delhi   Shanghai   Taipei   Toronto

With offices in
Argentina   Austria   Brazil   Chile   Czech Republic   France   Greece
Guatemala   Hungary   Italy   Japan   Poland   Portugal   Singapore
South Korea   Switzerland   Thailand   Turkey   Ukraine   Vietnam

Published by Oxford University Press, Inc.
198 Madison Avenue, New York, New York 10016
http://www.oup.com

Oxford is a registered trademark of Oxford University Press

Library of Congress Cataloging-in-Publication Data

Weston, Anthony, 1954–
   Creative problem-solving in ethics / by Anthony Weston.
      p. cm.
   Includes bibliographical references.
   ISBN-13:978-0-19-530620-0 (pbk. : alk. paper)
   ISBN 0-19-530620-1 (pbk. : alk. paper)
      1. Ethics. I. Title

BJ37.W47 2006
170—dc22   2005057728

9 8 7 6 5 4 3 2 1

Printed in the United States of America
on acid-free paper

CONTENTS

PREFACE

This is a "how-to" book about creativity in ethics. It turns out to be possible to take ethical problems, even hard and controversial and painful ethical problems, and to find some space in them, some room to move, maybe even some completely unsuspected and rather wonderful possibilities. Even in ethics we can "think out of the box."

True, this is not the key in which ethics is often played. Usually we're taught to think of ethics as a realm of judgment of deciding what is right and wrong. And of course such judgments are very important. Maybe it's even true that some situations really have no creative possibilities, and all we can do is "bite the bullet," as some moralists are fond of saying, and stick to difficult or seemingly harsh judgments come what may.

Through many years of thinking about ethical issues, though, I have learned that the insistence on judgment alone is very often a dead end. The most constructive ethical thinking may require us to look beyond the immediate controversies and difficulties. There are more creative possibilities even in the old familiar issues than we usually imagine. But we certainly won't find them if we don't look for them, and we even more certainly won't find them if we start out convinced that they can't be there in the first place. We need a more expansive view of ethics.

We also need a more inviting view of creativity. We are often tempted to think of creativity as a fixed trait, like eye color or body type, beyond anyone's ability to change. This book, I hope, will persuade you otherwise. The fact is that you can easily become more creative, using methods you know and trust. A complete genius, maybe, needs the genes (too), but almost all of us can do far better than we do now, partly because so few of us are trained in creative thinking at all. Even a few methods go a long way.

General readers will find this book useful, I hope, as an engaging, quick introduction to creative thinking in ethics. Teachers will wish to use it, I hope, in classrooms and workshops and, in particular, as a supplementary book for a university or high school class in ethics. Check out the "Notes and Sources" section at the end of the book for advice about how to use this book in such a class. It won't carry the whole class by itself, of course—you will need to go elsewhere for a history of ethics and a survey of its leading theories—but it will add an indispensable and sometimes even electrifying element. Don't slight the extensive exercises at the end of each chapter, which often contain new material as well.

This book has a sister, *Creativity for Critical Thinkers*, also published by Oxford University Press, offering similar creative tools but focused on practical creativity in general. This book also has cousins and aunts—other texts I have written for ethics and critical thinking courses, all of which might be helpful follow-ups to this one for certain purposes. For more on all of these books, see the "Notes and Sources" section at the end.

Conversations with colleagues, students, and classes far too numerous to list have shown me again and again how intriguing and liberating most people find the whole topic of creativity, especially in ethics. A sense of possibility and hope opens up, even when facing the stickiest or most troublesome problems. So I thank the many colleagues who have invited me to speak on these points and/or who have reported to me how helpful some of these tools have proved to their students. At Oxford University Press, my hat is off to my intrepid editor Robert B. Miller. Oxford's reviewers for this project include Christine Dinkins, Jeffrey Fry, Sharon Hartline, Stevens Wandmacher, and Dave Yount. My thanks to you all!

I also want to thank my students over recent years, who have provoked many themes and changes and are starting to contact me with big ideas that they have been working on, since the class, by themselves. And I thank YOU, now, as you start down the same path. I wish you the best of luck and heartily welcome all readers' comments, criticisms, and suggestions.

Anthony Weston
Durham, NC
weston@elon.edu

CREATIVE

PROBLEM-SOLVING

IN

ETHICS

1

CREATIVITY'S PROMISE IN ETHICS

POOR STUCK HEINZ

Say the word "ethics" today and the next word that comes to mind is usually "dilemma." We run into deep conflicts between certain values that do not seem to have any ready resolution. Abortion, capital punishment, genetic engineering, privacy versus security—all dilemmas. In all of these issues, we're told, we really have only a few choices: now, let's argue . . .

Hard choices are often reduced to dilemmas as well. In your study of ethics, you may have come across the so-called "Heinz dilemma," from the psychologist Lawrence Kohlberg:

> A woman was near death from cancer. One drug might save her, a form of radium that a druggist in the same town had

discovered. The druggist was charging $2000, ten times what the drug cost him to make. The sick woman's husband, Heinz, went to everyone he knew to borrow the money, but he could only get together about half of what it cost. He told the druggist that his wife was dying and asked him to sell it cheaper or let him pay later. But the druggist said "no"....

It is all too easy to agree with Kohlberg's assumption that Heinz really has but two choices: either to steal the drug or to watch his wife die.

Psychologists use this and other dilemmas to probe children's moral reasoning. Moral philosophers use them to illustrate and debate opposing ethical theories. But neither of these debates is our first concern here. We need to pose a more basic and less often asked question.

Are there really only two or a few sharply opposed options, either for Heinz or in any other of our supposed dilemmas? Or mightn't there just possibly be other options too? If we look at these problems with fresh eyes, might we even see possibilities in them that we can barely imagine now—maybe even new ways of approaching ethics itself? How far might a few creative problem-solving skills take us?

I ask my students to reapproach the Heinz dilemma with a few problem-solving tools. Can they imagine any other options for Heinz? Yes, they can. . . .

Maybe Heinz could offer the druggist something besides money, they say. Maybe he's a good piano tuner or a skilled gardener or a chemist himself. Why not trade his skills for the drug?

Or again, is this drug actually scientifically tested? Apparently not yet. In that case, maybe the druggist should pay "Ms. Heinz" for, in effect, volunteering in a drug test.

In one of my workshops, a group of health-care professionals even suggested that Heinz's wife break into the druggist's

WHAT IS CREATIVE PROBLEM-SOLVING?

Creative problem-solving is *the art of expanding possibility. It is the ability to cast a situation or challenge or problem in a new light and thereby open up possibilities in it that were not evident before.* It is the art of finding unexpected space in problems that may seem totally stuck to everyone else. It is the ability to think "out of the box" while the rest of us barely realize that we are *in* a box.

Creative problem-solving applies across the board, in all areas of life. But nowhere, right now, is it potentially so powerful as in ethics. Nowhere do we feel quite so stuck, quite so hopelessly at odds, or maybe just plain hopeless. And yet few types of issues are so important to our lives and the loves of others. Specifically, then, this book aims to teach creative problem-solving in ethics.

store herself and deliberately get arrested since (a useful fact to know) the state is legally required to provide medical care for prison inmates. Then she'd get the drug!

Also, Heinz and his wife don't live in a vacuum. What about public aid? Where are their family, friends, community? Think of the appeals you see in hardware stores and community groceries, complete with photos—a town rallying to buy an afflicted kid a bone marrow transplant, another chance at life. Just this summer my little hometown on the Wisconsin prairie raised $35,000 to buy a young man an artificial leg.

So Heinz *does* have a few more options, doesn't he? As does his afflicted but maybe not so helpless wife herself.

Notice too that many of these suggestions do much more than merely bring forward some dramatic and unexpected practical options for Heinz and his wife. They also invite us to think very differently about ethics itself. Just asking what Heinz should do overlooks the question of what *we* can do— and sometimes that is a lot more. Suppose our job, in the end, is not so much to judge this alleged dilemma as to figure out how we can help?

"GOOD MORNING, CHILDREN"

Here is another kind of ethical problem.

> A child in second grade underwent chemotherapy for leukemia. When she returned to school, she wore a scarf to hide the fact that she had lost all her hair. But some of the children pulled it off, and in their nervousness laughed and made fun of her. The child was mortified and that afternoon begged her parents not to make her go back to school. Her parents tried to encourage her, saying "The other children will get used to it, and anyway your hair will soon grow in again."

Let's say you are the teacher and this is your class. Ethics seems to make some pretty clear demands of you, doesn't it? You need to defend the mocked child. You can defend her with more or less skill—maybe by angrily lecturing the class about not hurting her feelings, maybe by telling a parable that makes the point more deftly—but the fact is (so it seems) that you need to "read the riot act." This is a time when even young children must take some responsibility and avoid causing hurt. Even second grade is not too early to learn the lesson.

Still, you can predict what the effects will be. A few children will get it, maybe. More are just going to "really feel sorry" for the poor kid, making both her and themselves terribly self-conscious. Others will retreat into sullenness. A few will put on a show of care but keep on taunting her behind your back, maybe even with sharper (because hidden) twists of the knife. And she herself will be even more embarrassed and hurt.

These are not the results you want either. But is there any other way? Are there alternative ways to approach the whole situation so that the class begins to learn the right kind of sensitivity and care but does not end up feeling strained or stuck?

Think about it. Really, what would *you* do? What *could* you do?

The story continues:

The next morning, when their teacher walked into class, all the children were sitting in their seats, some still tittering about the girl who had no hair, while she shrank into her chair. "Good morning, children," the teacher said, smiling warmly in her familiar way of greeting them. She took off her coat and scarf. Her head was completely bald.

After that, a rash of children begged their parents to let them cut their hair. And whenever a child came to class with short hair, newly bobbed, all the children laughed merrily, not out of fear but out of the joy of the game. And everybody's hair grew back at the same time.

This teacher did not lecture or moralize. Indeed, she did not say anything about "the problem" at all. Maybe she even carried on all day as if nothing unusual had happened. Yet in one stroke she did something dramatic and memorable and morally far more powerful than a lecture ever could be. We could say it like this: by shaving her own head, she invited the children into a new way of relating to the child with no hair. She showed them that there is something to do besides gape at her or feel sorry for her. The bald child was no longer a problem or an object of pity but became a playmate with options, just like she was before. Maybe even better.

Officially, we could say that the teacher invited the class into *solidarity* with the bald child, into voluntarily sharing her new look and a bit of her unusualness. This is the key moral lesson: we are all in this together. But the lesson is not taught with any heaviness. Quite the contrary, the teacher's genius was to make it fun—and to show the class a way that everyone can join in.

What a creative teacher! Would that all our teachers were like her—would that we were like her ourselves. And in all seriousness: why not?

A FEELING FOR POSSIBILITY

You begin to glimpse the possibilities for ethical problem-solving a little beyond—maybe more than a little beyond—what we're usually shown. Much of the rest of this book offers you some of the tools you need to think in this way. I want to make just one other point for now.

Ethical problem-solving is not just a matter of finding a way out of a specific, practical fix. It is also an occasion to better live out our values and, indeed, to better the world itself. That is the very essence of ethics!

Think again of those children at the moment their teacher first takes off her scarf and they see her shaved head. Confusion might be their first reaction. Then, quickly, the dawning realization of what they are being invited to: a completely new way of relating not just to the bald student but to each other. A stronger sense of values, of ethical possibility, comes into play, and it extends far beyond one child.

The implications also go far beyond this one situation. Last year I had a student who shaved his head, along with all of his family members, in solidarity with his mother who had lost her hair from chemotherapy. Whole city blocks have done it for a stricken neighbor. Fighting cancer is partly a lonely battle, but there is still a great deal that the rest of us can offer. We can all practice more solidarity.

CREATIVE PROBLEM-SOLVING AND THE REST OF ETHICS

Ethics requires diverse practical skills. Deliberate, careful, informed judgment is a piece of it. Attention to values, appropriate respect, self-awareness—all of these are necessary. All are challenging. All could use improvement, especially when we look around our society at present and see many moral debates generating so much more heat than light.

In short, there is much more to ethics than creative problem-solving—of course. Here we focus on creative problem-solving not because it is the only or even the most essential thing in ethics, but because it has a special promise, and because it is so often overlooked entirely.

Creativity is also not *unique* to ethics. But there is no reason to suppose that the only skills useful in ethics are the ones unique to it. In fact, by concentrating on certain intellectual challenges unique to ethics, we may slight the practical (and creative and imaginative) skills that are vital to ethics but not unique to it. So part of the aim of this book is to rejoin ethics to life skills, to put ethics into its rightful place.

Note finally that creative problem-solving is not specific to any particular school or type of ethics. You can be a utilitarian or a Kantian or even a relativist and put all the skills in this book to good use. You also can be either secular or religious. Many of the people we honor as wise decision-makers in the great religious traditions were exemplary creative and transformative thinkers. The wisest of the wise seldom just insist on some fixed judgment, come what may. Instead, they find some entirely unexpected but often wild and wonderful way around the problem, usually a way that builds solidarity or teaches a lesson as well. Think of King Solomon, for example, or the Sufi sages. So again: why not us?

In the Heinz case too, the most creative aim is not merely to find other ways out for Heinz and his wife, although that's a great place to start. A full-scale ethical resolution also challenges us to think about how we can prevent such dilemmas from even coming up in the first place. Forty-five million

Americans, right now, have no health insurance, a problem that both political parties sporadically address but that surely needs much more attention, however you think it might be resolved.

Here too we can and must take some responsibility for making the world a better place, not just judging someone else's (say, Heinz's) response to the world as it is. Myself, I can't imagine a more constructive or a more, finally, *ethical* approach than that!

FOR PRACTICE ☙

1. Here are some questions to think about.

- What comes to mind when you think of ethical problems? Do you welcome them as occasions for thinking and taking action, or do you expect only moralizing and argument and controversy? Why? What can you do to redirect the less constructive expectations—both your own and others'?

- Why do you think we are so seldom trained to think creatively —in any field, really, but least of all in ethics?

- Do you know some people who you think are especially good at creative problem-solving? Who are they? Talk to them; find out how they do it.

- What do you hope to gain from this book?

2. Creative thinking needs a limber mind: flexible, open, receptive. Try some serious mental stretching to warm up for the specific creative methods in the chapters to come. Here are a few thought-experiments to shake up some of our usual ethical preconceptions. Play with these—don't get tangled up in them—just exercise your imagination.

- Imagine that people lived forever. Would that be wonderful? Awful? How would we adjust? Would we totally switch identities every few hundred years? (Would you want to be the same person forever?) Would some people want out? What about you? What might be some of the effects on ethics as we know it?

- What if men got pregnant rather than (or in addition to) women? Would we think about sexual relations differently? What about abortion? What do you think Gloria Steinem meant when she said "If men got pregnant, abortion would be a sacrament"? (Is this an uneasy subject? Why?)

- What if there were a cheap, legal, "up" hallucinogenic drug with no side effects? What moral objections would remain?

- Try designing a company (or, if you're really ambitious, a whole economic or political system) without knowing what your own status will be within it. If you don't know whether you'll be a janitor or a CEO, a movie star or a bag lady, how will you set up your company's decision-making processes or your society's way of taking care of the needy?

- What if the world developed an international reconstruction and peace-keeping force? What skills would such a "force" call for? Who would join? (Think afresh here: it wouldn't have to be the young and able-bodied.) How would it work? How would the peace-makers and peace-keepers be trained?

- If you could use genetic engineering to totally remake human beings, how would you do it? Don't stop with everyday stylistic improvements, like adding gills so we can breathe under water and such. How about creating people without the capacity, say, for certain kinds of violence or fanaticism? How would you do that? Would there be losses as well as gains?

2

ETHICAL EXPLORATIONS

We now begin a survey of specific methods for creative problem-solving in ethics. First up are a number of modest types of *exploratory* thinking. Modest, yes—but don't underestimate them on that account. Slowly but surely they can open up unsuspected new ethical possibilities, and in the meantime they help prepare the ground for the more dramatic methods to come.

GET A FULLER PICTURE

Find out as much as you can about the specific situation that presents itself as an ethical problem.

Suppose someone put this question to you:

Terri Schiavo was on life support for 15 years, diagnosed as in a "persistent vegetative state" by most doctors. Was it ethical to remove her feeding tube and allow her to die?

You'd say (I hope): "Oh, I've heard of her—but isn't there more to the story?" This too-brief sketch gives us no idea of Schiavo's actual situation: how she ended up on life support with such brain damage, what her family situation was, if there was any hope of recovery, and what her own wishes might have been in this situation.

Better:

Terri Schiavo suffered severe brain damage from oxygen deprivation after cardiac arrest, leaving her on life support for 15 years in a condition diagnosed as an irreversible "persistent vegetative state" (PVS) by most doctors. Her husband, Michael, began efforts to remove her feeding tube and let her die, reporting that Terri had said several times that she would not want to be kept alive in such a state. Terri had made no formal declaration of her end-of-life wishes, though, and her parents disputed her husband's report. The diagnosis of PVS was also disputed by her parents and a few doctors and became the center of court battles and political debates. In the meantime, Michael became engaged to another woman, fathering two children with her, but was unable or unwilling to end his marriage to Terri. He also won a large malpractice award, partly to be devoted to continuing to take care of Terri, but soon afterward seems to have lost all hope for her. Her parents, meanwhile, declared in court that they would go to almost any lengths to keep her alive, including heart surgery and removal of her limbs.

The added detail makes the case stickier, yes—even gruesome. On the other hand, the very same detail opens up new possibilities that would not even have been on the horizon before. There's the point: we can already get much more creative than we could with just the first bare description.

If Schiavo had been kept alive, for example, various new therapies for PVS or near-PVS conditions might have been tried on her. If she recovered, wonderful; but even if not, testing new therapies might still "serve the cause of life," as some of her defenders were so eager to do. There would have been a better reason to keep her going.

The fuller description brings husband and parents into the picture too, which complicates things but again opens up new angles. My students argue, for instance, that Michael Schiavo needed to be able to move on. Fifteen years wedded to someone who cannot respond to you in any way is enough.

Terri Schiavo's parents seem to have taken a pretty extreme position too. So maybe what she really needed was a freshly appointed, and hopefully somewhat impartial, legal guardian. We have worked out ways of appointing relatively impartial mediators, even in very contentious cases. Why not extend them?

Finally, the fuller description also tells us that the case really turned on lack of clarity about Terri Schiavo's end-of-life wishes. Surely, then, we should promote "living wills," ways that people can declare their end-of-life wishes while still in full possession of their faculties. Apparently, many people did fill out living wills after the Schiavo controversy hit the news, but we'd do well to make it an expected thing. An ounce of prevention . . . well, you know.

WATCH FOR SUGGESTIVE FACTS

Suggestive facts are those that open up whole new ways of approaching a problem. Keep an eye peeled especially for them.

Case in point: a few years ago, I looked up the number of deaths caused by guns every year in the United States. The answer is about 30,000. This is a vastly disheartening number, in my view, but I already knew it was something like that. What surprised me was another figure that showed up along the way. Nearly half of these deaths are *suicides*. (Did you know that?)

This one number put the whole debate in a different light for me. True, the old argument is still there: the availability of guns makes impulsive killing easier, whether you kill yourself or someone else. But impulsive suicide is less likely than impulsive homicide: the inhibitions are greater, or maybe it's that we are just less likely to get murderously angry with ourselves. To me, the fact that 15,000 people a year deliberately kill themselves with guns suggests a need not so much for gun control as for suicide-prevention programs. And since suicide prevention must ultimately mean giving people compelling reasons to live, what it really means is finding ways to make life more exciting and rewarding for everyone. Thus I was led to a very new way of thinking about the whole issue.

Another example. In one of my classes a group of students was researching doctor-assisted suicide. They found a website that included biographies of the people that Dr. Jack Kevorkian had helped to die. It was a pro-Kevorkian website, making the case that assisted suicide can be a humanitarian act. And no doubt that is true. Many of those biographies, though, began to tell us another story.

We began to realize that Kevorkian became a last resort for many people because they not only were in pain but also lacked any kind of family or social support. The cruelest turn of all was one case in which the affected person could not take strong painkillers since he had no one to look after him when he was partly "knocked out." So he was in intense and unrelenting pain, and death looked like the only way out.

DON'T RUSH TO JUDGE

Just back from study in Bolivia, a student told me one day that the practice among the young Bolivian males he knew was to go to a prostitute for their sexual initiation. He was disturbed by this, and since he knew that I write books about ethics, he wanted my opinion.

I suppose he expected moral outrage. And I'm sure that moral outrage is appropriate, especially from the point of view of a society struggling to value women as full partners and equals. The problem is that the insistence on making such judgments pretty much closes down the discussion. Nothing else is explored; we think we've said everything that needs to be said.

For creative purposes, try a different attitude. Ask questions. Look for what might be *learned*, even from moral situations that puzzle you or make you uneasy. Again, the aim is to be more exploratory. Look for other angles and suggestive facts. Ask what practical challenges and opportunities the problem opens up. You don't have to somehow be nonjudgmental (this is important to emphasize for people who feel compelled or required to judge), but you *can* put your judgments to the side, at least for a little.

So my student and I kept talking. It turned out that when he had expressed his surprise and confusion to his Bolivian friends, they became curious to hear how sexual initiation works in the United States. And here, I thought, is a much more useful question. After all, we don't have much say over Bolivian men, do we, but we *can* make a difference in what we ourselves do. Do we really think that sexual initiation works very well in our own country? How do *we* teach young people about sex, anyway? Locker-room conversations? Movies? Pornography? How realistic or helpful or ethical are these?

How might we do better? Seriously: this is a real question. Never mind the Bolivians—*here* is where we might be able to make some creative moral progress. But we won't even take the first step if we think that our job is just to judge other people's practices and then, well, stop.

Judge if and when you must, then, but stay open to possibility too. And when you don't need to judge, or judge right away, *explore* instead. Learn to listen, ask good questions, and take your time.

Neither the pro nor the con side would say that in this kind of case death is the right answer. The real answer is to create communities of care such that no one is abandoned in this way. This is not quite what the website wanted to argue. Still, there it is anyway—a truly new option!

GET HELP

Other people naturally have different perspectives and different experiences than you do. They can also help bounce ideas around, sparking a new one or making a rough idea even better. Seek out friends who are willing to think in an exploratory spirit with you, and be such a friend to others.

Imagine a short dialogue on the issue of animal dissection in school.

A: I don't remember doing much dissection in my school days. Kids did bring in farm animals or organs from animals that had died on their farms.

B: Eeuw! You cut up an animal they knew?

C: It's better than cutting up animals that no one knew. With a farm animal you can at least hope that the animal had a decent life.

A: I wonder if we could think the same way about pets. B won't like it, but maybe people could donate their cats' and dogs' bodies for dissection too. And turtles and lizards and who knows what.

B: I don't like it. Have a little respect, why don't you?

D: My uncle donated his own body for dissection, for medical students to learn from. A lot of people are at least willing to be organ donors.

C: They know what will happen to their bodies. They do expect a certain respect, I think. So what if we did dissect our

---

BRAINSTORMING

Though we speak loosely of "brainstorming" for any attempt at creative thinking, the idea has a specific origin. Advertising executive Alex Osborne invented it (in 1939) as a deliberate process to facilitate creativity in groups. The key rule is to *defer criticism*. Welcome new ideas without immediately focusing on the likely difficulties and problems. Give new ideas, still barely hatched, enough space to develop and link up with others, to pass around the room, to provoke other ideas in turn.

The other guidelines for formal brainstorming work are:

- *Hitchhike on others' ideas.* Improve the last idea, or spark off it.
- *Wild ideas are OK.* No taboos; let the creative "juice" flow.
- *State ideas briefly, like telegrams.* This keeps the process flowing. You can always come back to expand the best ideas later.
- *Aim for quantity, not quality.* If you stop to try to develop the first good idea you have, you'll miss even better ideas that may come along after you've really gotten going.

---

friends' pets or our neighbors' farm animals? I bet it would teach us to be a little more respectful of *their* bodies too.

A: I also remember how much those farm kids had learned about the animals when they were *alive.* It makes you wonder why we have to do dissection at all. . . .

This is a creative little exchange. We catch sight of several new ideas. And it works for a very specific reason.

A, C, and D are consciously exploring, working toward some new possibilities together. They start out statements with "I wonder . . . ?" and "What if . . . ?" They bring in their own experiences. They nurture each other's ideas along. At the end, A even starts in on a new and more radical idea: that maybe dissection is not really the best way to learn about animals in the first place. Here is an entirely new line of thought that now invites its own development.

B is the foot-dragger. He seems to think that his job is only to judge or to react to the others' ideas, rather than add to them, develop or deepen them, or even offer an alternative. Reactions like B's could derail such a conversation. But notice the spirit in which the others take them here. They keep right on thinking in a more open-ended way, while making a few bows toward B along the way. They even take up B's theme of respect, but in an exploratory key. B helped out in spite of himself!

COMPARE AND CONTRAST

Do you know that there are some societies that will not tolerate leaving even a single person homeless? That assisted suicide is legal in the Netherlands (also in the state of Oregon) and the result is not a tidal wave of suicides? That for certain tribal peoples in North America, no decision was settled until the people had heard from the animals?

Even the wildest (to us) arrangements have probably been normal for some group of people somewhere and sometime. Probably even now. Did they learn anything from this? Couldn't we—from them?

Well, of course. We are not the only people to think long and hard about life-and-death decisions, marriage, punishment, or justice. All sorts of people have been thinking about ethical problems for a long time. All sorts of answers have been tried.

Another method for creative problem-solving in ethics, then, is simply to explore some of those other answers—that is, to explore other approaches to the same problems, at other times and places. Find out how quite different people and societies have dealt with these issues. You do not have to agree with them. Nor is the point to instantly produce workable solutions. The point is to free up our thinking: to look at our problems from new directions, once again; to widen our sense of possibility.

You may discover that certain problems that seem utterly stuck to us may not be problems at all for other people or at other times. Abortion, for example, one of the United States' most divisive and painful and seemingly fundamental social conflicts over the past thirty years, is barely an issue in many other countries (though now we're exporting it) and historically was not much of an issue even here. (It may feel like the abortion debate has been going on forever, but that is only because most of us aren't that old—and because we haven't really gotten anywhere.) Moreover, even when abortion became an issue, conservatives originally *favored* relaxed abortion laws, while liberals had their doubts (check it out).

By itself all of this background doesn't suggest any solutions, of course, but it does give us a sense of possibility and movement. Things aren't necessarily as stuck as they look.

That the Dutch have survived the legalization of marijuana probably tells us something about the possibilities here at home. And what about alcohol? Many countries have both fewer restrictions on alcohol and dramatically fewer drunk-driving deaths. Why? How can we learn from this?

Or take the much-fought-over issue of marriage. In Australia, many couples live together in so-called "de facto" marriages; they seem to do about as well as the more official kind. The French have extended civil unions to same-sex couples, with the unexpected result that many opposite-sex couples also opt for them. There seems to be a market for alternative sorts of partnership.

Some conservatives are now promoting a new kind of marriage themselves, Covenant Marriage, which is stricter than the usual kind of marriage. This too suggests that the nature of marriage is not a settled question. Different arrangements are possible. Instead of struggling over the definition of one kind of marriage, maybe we should, well, diversify.

Comparing and contrasting may take some research. You need to look for contrasting views and approaches—that is, contrasting both to our own and to each other. Find the practical details, too. How do the French civil contracts work? How do the Dutch regulate marijuana? (It's interesting: you can't buy it for home use; it is available only in a coffeehouse-like setting, in small amounts, and regulated by the equivalent of a bartender, which might, again, be suggestive about how we could treat liquor as well.)

So many questions! How *do* native peoples manage to listen to the wolves and even the rivers and stones? How can it be that very potent hallucinogens are widely used but not addictive in intact indigenous cultures? Really, *how*? The detail alone is often fascinating, the practical lessons are sometimes vital, and above all we may come back to our own problems with an entirely new set of ideas.

FOR PRACTICE 🖐

Pick some ethical issues of concern to you to explore, and try all of the methods in this chapter. Look for a fuller picture, look for new and especially suggestive facts about those issues, find willing friends and practice brainstorming, and compare and contrast. Here are a few issues you might consider.

- Is dissection the best (only?) way to really learn about animals? Or put it the other way around: what is really most important to know about other animals or our own bodies? Why? (For example, what do you really need to know in order to be a good doctor?) Suppose you had to design a biology curriculum that did not involve dissection at all. Where would you start?

- Our children's, maybe even our own, moral and personal role models tend to be movie stars, athletes, political leaders (?). Who might be more suitable? More specifically, what more suitable role models might also have the allure and the visibility of the movie star, etc.? Might we have to create them? How?

- What might the elderly do with their time? How could society be restructured to respond to their needs and to better enable them to speak to ours? How about a system of adoptive grandparents, as some of my students have suggested? And what other opportunities might aging represent? Must even selective memory loss necessarily be viewed as a mental failing? Could it even be regarded as an *advantage*? How?

- We're told that there is a dilemma between birth mothers' right to privacy and adoptees' right to know where they came from. Maybe so. But maybe not. We won't really know until we look at actual evidence. Some states, for example, allow adoptees to find out who their birth mothers are. Others have established a registry so that those birth mothers and adoptees who wish to be found can be. How have these and other arrangements worked? What would be some useful further experiments?

- We say that drugs offer an escape from school or work or just life itself. But this leads to other questions. Why do so many people need such an escape in the first place? And what can we do about school or work or life itself so that such an escape is less tempting? Aren't there less lethal ways to make life more joyful and interesting?

- What happens when personal ethics conflict with organizational practices: say, in business or the military or government? How could such conflicts be better handled? Are there new and creative ways to deal with the problem of "whistleblowing"— and the kinds of problems that lead to the need for whistleblowing in the first place?

- Rich countries try to help less well-off countries when natural disasters strike (earthquakes, hurricanes, etc.). What about also helping to overcome the underlying causes of poverty itself? Meanwhile, aren't there some ways in which *we* need *their* help? What would a system of truly mutual aid look like?

• We are consuming food, energy, and other natural resources at unsustainable rates, and what kind of world we will pass on to our descendants is becoming increasingly uncertain as a result. What to do?

3

ETHICAL
PROVOCATIONS

Creative ethical thinkers also attempt some rather more dramatic kinds of exploration—methods of mental *provocation* as well. These are also, as it happens, the favorites of most creativity experts.

INVITE EXOTIC ASSOCIATIONS

For better or worse, we are creatures of habit. If we always had to think things through from the beginning, we'd barely be able to get out of bed in the morning. But mental habits can also become mental ruts. We can get so stuck in certain ways of thinking that we barely are aware of them at all, so it's especially hard to realize that there may be entirely new possibilities right next door, so to speak, but invisible to us still. And therefore the task of creative thinking is to wake us up to them—even abruptly, as sometimes it may have to be.

Already in the last chapter you were watching for suggestive facts and drawing on your friends for their different experiences and ideas. They can be sources of unfiltered and unfamiliar ideas. By way of a full-scale method, you can now take the same process much farther.

Try this: generate a set of prompts or "provocations" in a random way, and then free-associate from there. That is, invite—even force—*exotic associations*.

For such "provocations" your source can literally be *anything*: a dictionary, an overheard conversation, some images from your house or a book, a mystery, a magazine. If you're using words, it's best to have a source with a varied and rich vocabulary—a good classic writer, maybe—but in a pinch you can even take words or images from billboards along the freeway or by turning on the car radio for two seconds, as I sometimes do if I am using this method while driving. Or look around the room you are in right now (or out the window, or try to remember last night's dreams, or . . .).

The aim is simply to produce as truly different and varied a set of new ideas as you can. Now you really have a new, unfiltered stimulus for your thinking—from outside whatever "box" you are currently in. Right away something fresh. Then put it together with the problem you are thinking about. Don't censor, edit, or judge. Give each association, however crazy it may seem, some time. What new possibilities, what new ways of thinking, might it suggest?

Take the problem of litter—of thrown-out cans and bottles. We're used to hearing all about our responsibility to use trashcans, to recycle. Well, it's true, we should. But is that it?

Nothing more to say? Could we think farther and more creatively about this problem that is so familiar it's boring?

Let us try some exotic associations. Looking around, just past my desk, I see my houseplants. Alright then: could the image of a houseplant (that's random, eh?) suggest some new associations, different ways of thinking about discarded cans and bottles?

Now I free-associate. Hmm . . . well, houseplants do make the room more beautiful. So maybe we could start making cans and bottles that are the same? Art made with "junk" can be wonderful, but we could imagine something more systematic, like juice containers made of differently colored plastic that can be joined Lego-style into kids' play structures or (who knows?) stained-glass windows. Paper wrappers that could be used for origami?

Plants are also food—one way or another nearly everything we eat comes from plants. Well then, what if we associate edibility with can and bottle litter? Any usable ideas there?

How about . . . um, edible cans and bottles?

It sounds crazy at first—new ideas quite likely will. Some of them no doubt *are* crazy. But this one has some promise. Picture it: you could eat your food, then eat the wrapper to top it off. Drink your coffee and then down the cup too. Actually, we do this very thing already with some foods: think of tacos or pita wraps or, for heaven's sake, ice cream cones. So edible food "wraps" are not even that unfamiliar. Couldn't we extend the idea?

Maybe there's something to this exotic-association method after all?

Plants . . . gardens? Bottles and cans in the garden? This may provoke yet another idea: bottles and cans as *fertilizer?* At least we could make cans and bottles so that they biodegrade really fast, couldn't we?

Keep going. Suppose we add some fertilizer and grass seeds or wildflower seeds or something and then, rather than discouraging "litter," encourage it instead. Don't stick those cans and bottles in the boring old bins; just throw them onto some bare ground, thank you. Or into your garden. Cans of tomato juice could have tomato seeds in them, apple juice bottles could contain apple seeds. . . .

We could go farther with this, but you see the point. Even with a couple of seemingly unpromising associations, we are now thinking *way* out of the box about the litter issue. No more guilt-tripping about recycling—just eat the stuff. There's creativity for you!

NO FILTERS

How to pick useful provocations? The key point is that you can't preselect them according to your hunches about what would be most relevant or helpful. That is exactly what you are trying to *find out* in the first place. No—just try some different prompts and see what comes of them.

A good rule is to stick with any prompt, no matter how unpromising it seems, for at least three minutes (and use a timer: three minutes may be longer than you think). You won't know what you can get from it until you try.

Trust the process. Don't try to edit or filter or prejudge it— just give yourself over to it. Free-associating on the Heinz dilemma, for instance, I turned to the dictionary for random words, and the first word I found was "oboe." "Oboe?" I said to myself. "You've got to be kidding!" Then I thought, "Well, an oboe is a musical instrument; an oboe-like instrument is used to charm cobras in India; maybe Heinz could somehow charm the druggist?"

How? Well, I'm not sure, but it seems worthwhile for Heinz at least to talk to the druggist some more. We shouldn't assume the druggist is a completely boxed-in automaton, any more than Heinz is.

Or again, people play oboes . . . it is a skill . . . people have skills . . . Heinz has skills. . . . From here it might occur to us that Heinz could barter other things besides money for the drug.

The next word I found was "Leaf." "Turn over a new leaf"? "Read leaves"? (Hmm . . . foretelling the future, as people used to do with tea leaves? How do we know that this drug is any good?) Use leaves instead of drugs? (Are there herbal remedies?)

If you absolutely must shape your prompts, seek out the wildest ones you can find. Oboes, leaves, OK—but also try some *really* wild provocations, like going to the moon, lassoing a dinosaur, or the year 5000. Skydiving? The circus?

GO TO EXTREMES!

Rather than looking at small improvements to an existing, complex ethical problem, another creative method produces its provocations by *going to extremes.*

One way is to imagine what would be a *perfect* solution to your problem, the absolutely best possible solution. Then, once you've imagined an absolutely ideal outcome, however "unrealistic" it might be (or seem), you can work your way back to a more realistic idea from there. In short, make your very first imaginative step a really big one. It's easier to tone it down later than to ramp up a timid little half-step idea into something bigger.

Take the drunk-driving problem. One "perfect" solution might be a world in which drinking and driving cannot mix.

Put positively: suppose everyone who gets into cars is (*must* be) optimally alert, sober, ready.

Sure, it's not likely to happen. But even to visualize it points us in new directions. Maybe there are alternative solutions besides the obvious tactics of more road patrols and stricter laws. There are devices available that will a lock a car's ignition if the driver fails an in-car breathalyzer test. Some courts require them for DWI offenders. A simpler and more widely applicable strategy would be to just make it harder to start a car. Certainly it could take more alertness or coordination than just turning a key. (Flight of fancy: I imagine a quick video game, or maybe you have to beat your car's computer at speed chess; but of course we could set a similar standard by more boring mechanical means. Suppose you need to use both hands in a somewhat complex movement....)

We could also promote a stronger ethic of driving. That's a process already under way: ten years ago, there were no such things as "designated drivers." So what's next? What would you suggest? Maybe rewarding nondrinkers with new kinds of fabulous but nonintoxicating drinks, by design incompatible with liquor?

Thinking about "perfect" solutions might provoke some social creativity too. Suppose that bars provided taxi service to all patrons—that is, not just those patrons who wanted a taxi and were prepared to pay for it but *all* patrons, as a matter of course and part of the price of the drinks. Bars might not even be allowed to maintain parking lots: they could use the saved money for taxis or, as my students have suggested, "bar buses" that take young people to and from dorms or homes. The social meaning of drinking would itself change (again). Interesting.

Another way to "go to extremes" is to deliberately *reverse* certain features of the problem. Take the dissection issue again, for instance. Think of its elements: students, curriculum, teachers, the specimen animal, etc. Perhaps these could be interestingly reversed? What if . . . I don't know . . . maybe *students dissect the teacher*? Come to think of it (which is really what we're doing, isn't it—helping ourselves to come to think of new things?) what if the specimen animal dissects *you*?

The moralist in you may be shocked, and you may want to quickly disavow any morally questionable or otherwise seemingly gross sorts of options. But again, don't. Obviously we are not going to actually dissect a teacher or ourselves, but couldn't this thought, taken as a provocation, open up some other interesting ideas, just around the corner?

One interesting new question is, "How much can we learn from looking carefully at our own or each others' bodies— maybe about blood flow or muscles and leverage?" Think of how exercise machines are designed to isolate muscle groups. Truly, we could learn anatomy by paying attention to our own living bodies. And notice: studying our own bodies, live, would mean that we wouldn't need to use animals at all. Or we could study animals live, rather than dead, as well. Now there's a practical and fresh idea!

Yet another way to go to extremes is to *exaggerate* some aspect of the problem before you. Take some feature of it and make it as extreme, as overdone, as you can. Then stand back and see what new ideas or perspectives it might provoke.

How do you exaggerate dissection? What I visualize is somehow literally going inside the animal. Not merely by methodically disassembling its remains with a knife in a lab, but actually jumping inside its body.

Wild, eh? Impossible, of course. But hold on. Couldn't we once again move from this "crazy" idea to something more workable? How about computer simulation? In fact, doesn't the computer open up all sorts of nifty possibilities, like

---

PUTTING THE TOOLS TOGETHER

Exotic associations, going to extremes, brainstorming—and other methods to come—are distinct methods, though all of them have the exploratory spirit. This does not mean that they can only be used separately. Quite the contrary: many times they are best used together. An exotic association might push you to extremes, or vice versa. Comparing and contrasting will give you a new range of suggestive facts and associations. Don't suppose you have to keep them separate—that's only useful by way of introducing them, and maybe sometimes if you want to choose one or the other for purposes of jump-starting some creative thinking.

You may be brainstorming in a group. Fine: deliberately use random provocations or "go to extremes." Groups can get in ruts too, just like you or me when thinking on our own. So look for some random source, a good book maybe, or exaggerate or reverse some aspect of the problem—anything to loosen up a little, to break the ice or get the group onto some new track. A good facilitator should know when to pull out a new technique. Likewise, if you are tackling a problem alone, try a variety of methods to see which works the best for you (this time).

---

shrinking yourself down to the size of a cell and touring a living body through the veins (or lymphatic system, bile ducts, etc.) or tracking changes in the body over time or in different activities (sleep, exercise, sex, alarm, etc.)?

Along these lines, here's my suggestive fact for the day: it turns out that there already are jellybean-sized "camera pills" that can pass through the stomach and intestines scanning for tumors or infections. Next up are even smaller and remote-controlled versions that can also collect cell samples and administer medication. Soon enough we should be able to send them through the blood as well.

So really, in the long run, we might not even need computer simulations: we can tour our own bodies *in fact*. We need only

> ## HOW TO EXPAND YOUR OPTIONS—SUMMARY
>
> - *Get a Fuller Picture.* Find out as much as you can about the specific situation; watch for new possibilities to come up.
> - *Watch for Suggestive Facts.*
> - *Get Help.* find people to brainstorm difficult issues with you.
> - *Compare and Contrast.* Explore how the same problem is treated in other places and times.
> - *Invite Exotic Associations.* Seek unfiltered "provocations" in random words, analogies, or images; free-associate from there.
> - *Go to Extremes.* Start with "perfect" solutions and work toward realism; reverse or exaggerate key features of the problem.

expand the use of "camera pills" from diagnosis into the schools. We can explore our very own bodies as living laboratories. Classes can explore each other's stomachs, bad knees, you name it, from the inside. Kids will love this! And who would need dissection then?

FOR PRACTICE ☙

1. Begin by practicing the methods from this chapter on problems that are not yet ethical. What about, say, getting yourself out of the bed in the morning? Increasing voter turnout? Reducing kids' time in front of the TV? Lack of inexpensive travel options? Boredom?

Or suppose an elephant (or python or pack of cats, or . . .) has escaped in your neighborhood. Figure out five (or ten, or more) ways it can be recaptured. Or figure out ten (or twenty, or more) ways to get water out of a glass without moving or damaging the glass.

For more challenges like these, look at the "For Practice" sections in Chapters 2 and 3 of this book's sister, *Creativity for Critical Thinkers.*

Now consider some social issues—just don't take really big ones right away. Any new ideas for slowing down speeders? What about, say, five original ways to help people make better marriages? To improve teen–parent relations? To keep politicians honest?

2. Imagine that you are a scriptwriter for a movie studio. Your assignment is to create new scripts dealing with some emerging ethical issues, such as assisted suicide, human cloning, or the problem of environmental racism and (in)justice (that is, that disadvantaged communities often also have to deal with more waste dumps, toxic pollution, and bad air).

But you're not writing documentaries here. You've been hired for your ingenuity and flair at *drama*. You need to set up a problem and build your story around people engaging that problem. Make it hard, so that for a long time it is not clear how any effort to deal with the problem could possibly succeed. And then carry us through to some solutions with unexpected and creative twists. This is Hollywood, after all: you need to tie up the loose ends of your plot in a satisfying but unexpected and dramatic ending. It's ethics too, though, so you'll want a transformative resolution that maybe even invites us to think about ethics itself in a different way.

Tough job. On the other hand, remember that you do have some control over the plot. The general problem area is given, but, like a good mystery writer, you can imagine a specific situation and build the eventual resolution into the unfolding story. Have fun, and use the methods in this chapter.

If you're not keen on coming up with plots on your own, here is a variation on this exercise, a few brief scenarios to use as starting points.

A TV reporter investigating a new make of car discovers that the car is much more dangerous than people suspect. The manufacturer may or may not know of the dangers. She pitches the story to her editor, who not so gently reminds her that the car's manufacturer advertises lavishly on her station.

No way: the story will not run, and if she pursues it, she will be out of a job. Meanwhile, the car becomes a best seller, and several of her close friends and family members buy one.

A resistance fighter is captured by the police forces of a thoroughly nasty dictatorship. She is offered the following choice: reveal the names of other resistance fighters or you will be executed and then, when other fighters are eventually captured, they will be told that you betrayed them.

Three mountain climbers, roped together, have become trapped. One has fallen and is dangling off a cliff with no footholds available. A second, trying to rescue the first, has also fallen. The last has the only solid foothold. She is slowly weakening. Night is falling. If she cuts the other two loose, they will fall to their deaths. If she doesn't, all three look doomed. What should she do?

Scenarios like these can be found in many popular ethics texts (mine included). However, these texts present these scenarios as occasions for comparing and debating ethical judgments. In this exercise you are invited to take them in a different spirit. Use them as starting points for your script. *Start* with them as the grim dilemmas that we usually imagine, but don't end there. What other options might there be? Show us some other dramatic and unexpected possibilities. Are these situations really as stuck as they look?

3. This book began with a case that philosophers have found so difficult that it became a classic example of an ethical dilemma. Here is another—we could probably even say *the* other—famous modern moral dilemma. The French philosopher Jean-Paul Sartre described a young man in occupied Paris during World War II who came to him for advice.

His father was on bad terms with his mother, and, moreover, was inclined to be a collaborationist [that is, he cooperated with the Nazis]; his older brother had been killed in the German offensive of 1940, and the young man, with somewhat immature but generous feelings, wanted to avenge him. His mother lived alone with him, very much upset by the half-treason of her husband and the death of her elder son; the boy was her only consolation.

The boy was faced with the choice of leaving for England and joining the Free French forces—that is, leaving his mother behind— or remaining with his mother and helping her to carry on. He was fully aware that the woman lived only for him and that his going off—and perhaps his death—would plunge her into despair. He was also aware that every act that he did for his mother's sake was a sure thing, in the sense that it was helping her to carry on, whereas every effort he made toward going off and fighting was an uncertain move which might run aground and prove completely useless. . . . He was faced with two very different kinds of action: one concrete, immediate, but concerning only one individual; the other concerned an incomparably vaster group, a national collectivity, but for that very reason was dubious, and might be interrupted en route.

Imagine that this young man came to you for some help in this situation. Do you see any options for him? Take your time, and use the methods in this chapter.

4

REFRAMING ETHICAL PROBLEMS

We have been speaking of problem-*solving*. Sometimes, though, there are more creative ways to address ethical problems—better ways to make all-around progress on them —than "solving" them in the most straightforward way. So some major steps remain to be taken in our survey of methods for creativity. This chapter introduces three alternative ways of addressing ethical problems.

REVISIT OUTLYING PARTS OF THE PROBLEM

Remember the child who has lost her hair and is being teased by her classmates? Naturally enough in our problem-solving we tend to focus on *her*, on the bald child herself. She's the problem, right?

It was her teacher's genius to look somewhere else. The teacher didn't first ask how she might change the bald child (wig? psychotherapy?) or how she might change the other students (lecture? shame?). She first asked how she might change *herself*. It turned out that her end of things could actually be varied much more dramatically and fruitfully. She shaved her own head.

The general rule is to revisit *all* the parts of a problem, not just the one or two that currently fill the screen. Each aspect can be varied and questioned: new possibilities will come up. It may well be that some other aspect of a problematic situation, pushed into the background at the moment, offers us a way to go forward while the current routes seem blocked.

Emmanuel Evans ran a department store during the 1940s and 1950s in my city, Durham, North Carolina. The store had an attached, sit-down cafeteria. Segregation-era laws forbade the seating of black people in such an eating establishment. They had to stand, get their food, and go outside to eat. Evans was unwilling to treat his black customers in this way. But what to do? The direct approach—seating black people in defiance of the law—would quickly end with fines and jail (remember, this was before the Civil Rights movement and the era of mass civil disobedience). Closing the cafeteria served no one's interests either.

So the direct approach was blocked. What about an indirect approach? Mightn't the problem yield to an approach from another angle? Think about it.

Naturally, we first imagine changing things for the black customers. But suppose things could be changed for the *white* customers instead? Couldn't white people (also) *stand?* Evans finally realized that he could just remove all the tables, so that no one was seated. No law was broken, but a powerful statement was made. His cafeteria became the first desegregated eating place in town. And Evans, by the way, later became one of Durham's best-loved mayors.

For another example, take the debate over the censorship of sexually explicit material. No doubt there is much to say for banning or strictly controlling many kinds of pornography, and this is naturally where our thinking goes first. Once again, though, by thinking only of what we wish to ban, we are looking at only one aspect of the problem, and when we run up against free-speech protections, we're pretty much stuck. So look around—is more progress possible on some other aspects of this problem?

Here's one answer. One of the worst effects of treating sex as "dirty" has been that mainstream culture has virtually abandoned the imagination of sex to the movie industry, advertisers, and pornographers. We can do better than this! As one writer argues:

> If pornography becomes outlawed (again), it, like prostitution, will only come to represent the notion that sex is dirty, even more than it does today. What is needed instead is the development of sexual materials that take the best of the pornographic tradition—sexual openness, exploration, and celebration—and add to these egalitarian values, imagination, artfulness, respect for ourselves, and respect for the power and beauty of sex itself.

In short, rather than simply wishing to repress what we don't like, we might consider better promoting what we *do* like—perhaps learning something in the process as well. It sounds to me like a rather exciting thing to do. And it is a lovely invitation to all of us, from conservative religious people to gay activists and even, yes, moviemakers, to offer *positive* visions —which is, once again, surely exactly what ethics ought to be doing!

THE OLD STOICS RETHINK HAPPINESS

How can we really be happy, or anyway more happy, in a world that all too often doesn't cooperate?

Looked at in the familiar way, happiness is a matter of having satisfied needs and desires. Most people therefore naturally tend to seek happiness by trying to fulfill their desires—to get what they want. Sometimes it works, sometimes it doesn't.

You may ask, "What else can we do?" *C'est la vie.* But now that I have been urging you to revisit other aspects of the problem, you might take a question like that a little more seriously. Could there be another approach?

Well, yes. The old Stoics pointed out that there are (at least) two ways, not just one, to live a life of satisfied desire. One is to satisfy all your (many) desires. The other is *not to have too many desires*—to deliberately desire only a few things, and things that are readily attainable.

That's certainly a different way of thinking, isn't it? Especially in a culture in which we are saturated in advertising, whose very function after all is to make us want more and more things we don't need, keeping all but the richest in a state of perpetual dissatisfaction (and I'm not so sure about them either). The whole idea of Stoicism is to offer a side door out of this house of mirrors. At the very least, it would be a wise thing to *reconsider* our desires, don't you think?

THE PROBLEM IS THE OPPORTUNITY

Another way of reframing problems is to take the ethical problem before us not as a difficulty to be overcome or gotten rid of but as an actual *opportunity* to be welcomed. Believe it or not. Instead of trying to get rid of "the problem," we can ask how we can make *use* of it—and not, or not just, as a "problem" but as a resource, as a solution already, if we can just find the right use for it and reframe the situation in front of us.

The method itself is very simple. Take any problem. Seek out the very core of the difficulty. Identify it, and state it clearly. Then ask yourself, "Can I think of any way in which this 'problem' might actually be *welcomed? Are* there *opportunities* in it? For what?"

Case in point: go to any old-age home and you will find people desperate for something constructive to do. There are some organized games and other activities, but the feeling is simply that time is being filled. Professionals are even trained and hired to find ways to keep the occupants busy—disguising what we normally assume to be the simple fact that really there *is* nothing for them to do.

You could think of some creative responses in the usual problem-solving mode. Adapting computer games for older people? (A rather large market, you'd think.) Or how about more crafts?

These are fine ideas, but they are also still entirely in the mode of solving the problem as it stands: filling up old people's time. A seriously creative approach would be to ask what their unfilled time is an *opportunity* for. Is it really a problem at all, or more like a *resource?*

Ask the question in this way and everything looks different. Of course it is a resource! Obviously most older folks aren't going to be blazing wilderness trails or hanging telephone lines or sheet rock or something, but surely there are many ways that they can contribute. Here we have skilled, experienced, patient people, anxious for some constructive work. Hmm ... why should it be hard to hook their abilities up with community needs?

Nursing homes could be connected with public libraries, for example, and the occupants could take over cataloguing and book care. It's good, careful, and quiet work—plus they'd have all the books and videos they want close at hand.

Older people could take over or create community histori-
cal museums. In almost all tribal and traditional communities,
the elders are the custodians of the community's history. They
carry the memories and instruct the young. Why are we letting both the elders and the history slip away?

Even better, we know that many young parents are desperate for good-quality daycare. Once again, buildings are built
(sometimes right next to the nursing home) where staff are
trained and hired, this time to find ways to keep the children
busy and maybe even teach them something—hopefully not
just watching TV. But why not bring the very young and the
very old *together* in a setting in which both can help each
other? The old can tell their stories to the very people who
above all love stories. And the young can help tend to the
needs of the old, learning something of life cycles and of service in the process.

Reframing problems in this way does take some imaginative work. Usually it will not be obvious at first what the seem-
ing problem could possibly be an opportunity for (except for
pulling your hair out). Often it will seem silly even to ask.
Patience, patience . . . just ask anyway, "Even so, what *could* it
be an opportunity for?" Use the tools from previous chapters
to help generate some concrete ideas. Stick with it (remember
the three-minute rule from Chapter 3). Don't be blinded just
because a situation is *labeled* a "problem" (or "dilemma").
There will still be possibilities in it. The essential step is your
willingness to look for them—your expectation that maybe,
just maybe, there might be something to be found.

THINK PREVENTION

We understand the logic of prevention when it comes to
health. Everyone knows that it's better to take vitamins and

exercise than to wait until you get sick and then have to deal with the illness. We don't always act on this knowledge, for a variety of reasons, but we do know it.

In ethics, the strategy could be the same: look *before* or *behind* a problem as it is usually presented. Don't just take the problem for granted. Instead, consider whether it even needs to come up in the first place. Ask whether a few small changes a few steps back can change everything about the problem here and now. This is a third method for radically reframing problems.

When I began studying ethics (let's just say it was some time back), Terri Schiavos were everywhere. People ended up brain-dead but physically still alive on hospital respirators, and families would plead with one voice (unlike in Schiavo's case) to let them die. But the law wasn't clear. There were no moral precedents, so typically such patients were kept going, sometimes for years, breaking the family's bank as well as their hearts.

Things have changed since then. We have made some progress. And what changed is chiefly one thing: living wills. Once people declare themselves in advance on the subject—usually to say that they do not want to be kept alive in such a condition—the lawyers are satisfied, and the entire debate has calmed down immensely. Schiavo's case is now the exception rather than the rule, and as we've noted, it is prompting even more people to make their wishes clear in advance—all to the good.

Recently I heard a similar story about fertility clinics. When these clinics started storing couples' fertilized embryos, they found themselves in huge battles when couples split up. Which partner "owned" the embryos? You could imagine a lot of ethical headshaking and decades of contentious cases winding their ways through the courts. The clinics, wisely, took a very different and preventive approach. Now, before they create any embryos at all, they ask each couple to designate one or the other as the embryos' "owner" in the event of divorce. No more problem!

Or again, the best approach to the challenge of recycling may be to reduce or eliminate the need to recycle in the first place, especially by redesigning products and packaging so that they never become "junk" at all. "Precycling," it's called, rather than recycling. Make products that biodegrade rapidly or have other attractive uses—building blocks maybe, collectibles, toys (think of the marketing angles there). Or require manufacturers to take them back (the European Union already does this)—*then* we'll get reusable parts in a hurry.

We've considered ethical dilemmas such as the Heinz dilemma. To that dilemma, surely, the best response is to try to keep the whole problem from arising at all. The whole point of "catastrophic" medical insurance is to help people out when facing medical costs that can quickly spiral far beyond nearly anyone's ability to pay. How to extend coverage to everyone who needs it is the key question. Precisely insofar as Heinz's wife really is "stuck," then, *we* need to be figuring out how to keep such tragedies from even occurring.

Consider, finally, one other textbook sort of ethical dilemma:

In the aftermath of a mid-ocean collision, thirty people are crowded into a lifeboat meant for ten. Seas are frigid and high, and rescue appears unlikely for a long time. There is food for only a few people, and the lifeboat probably cannot even remain afloat so dangerously overloaded. Should some people be asked to jump overboard to save the rest—or thrown out if they don't agree?

Sometimes this scenario is even made into a teaching game (!?).

Some philosophers argue that there simply is no ethical answer in this kind of case—that ethics is not for such

---

AN OBJECTION AND RESPONSE

Traditional moralists may complain that reframing problems, especially in a preventive way, really just avoids the problems. It's evasive. One of my students described it as like "tap dancing around" the dilemma. We haven't really solved anything, he said.

It's an important objection. I want to respond in several ways.

First: from a practical point of view, just exactly what is wrong with avoiding problems? As a hypothetical or intellectual exercise, of course you may want to take up the familiar ethical dilemmas in their own terms. But most people come to ethics with a different purpose. We want to live intelligent and sensitive lives. If we can make a way that is not strewn with "dilemmas," especially insoluble ones, isn't that just what we should want? Surely the ability to creatively recast ethical dilemmas should be a prime ethical skill.

We can go farther. Why is the objector entitled to be so assertive about what "the" problem actually is in the first place? Who says "the" real problem must be the dilemma? A more creative approach, anyway, questions this very self-confidence. Why mightn't we say that "the" issue is finding a decent alternative that acknowledges and integrates different values that appear to conflict but might not necessarily conflict if things were arranged better?

Maybe the problem in such cases is not so much intellectual or theoretical as it is imaginative. It's a practical and reconstructive challenge, a "dance" of its own kind. So just who is *really* avoiding "the" problem?

---

extreme cases, where every civilized bet is off and no ethics should even be expected to have an answer. Stick to the less dramatic but real ethical challenges of our lives, they say.

I have a lot of sympathy with this response. Still, clearly, the only decent answer is to require all ships to carry adequate numbers of lifeboats. Of course, this won't resolve the quandary if somehow you do end up in an overcrowded lifeboat. What we can and must do, once again, is to try to prevent such

WAYS TO REFRAME ETHICAL PROBLEMS—SUMMARY
The methods in this chapter ask you to rethink problems themselves as they are usually presented. How can they be redefined? What are their causes? Are they necessarily even problems at all? • *Revisit Outlying Aspects of the Problem.* Mentally vary *all* the changeable aspects of a problematic situation, not just the ones right now in the spotlight. • *The Problem Is the Opportunity.* Could the very situation that seems to be such an ethical problem actually be an ethical *opportunity* if viewed in the right way? • *Think Prevention.* How can this problem be headed off before it even comes up?

situations from even arising in the first place. Sometimes prevention is not only the best medicine—it is the only medicine.

FOR PRACTICE 𝔖

1. Use the tools in this chapter, as well as Chapters 2 and 3, to take up a range of current ethical issues. The list at the end of Chapter 2 would be a good place to start: drugs, the moral status of animals, international aid, the environment, and others. Go back to those problems now and see how much farther you can go. Check out your daily newspaper, or your ethics text, for many more.

2. Here are several further moral issues on which to use your full set of creativity methods, with special emphasis on those introduced in this chapter.

   • Defenders of the death penalty say that murderers forfeit their own right to life, that execution is the only really "proportionate" penalty for murder, and that the threat of execution deters would-be murderers from committing the act. Opponents argue that if cold-blooded killing is wrong, it is wrong when the state does it too; that life in prison is at least as appropriate a penalty; and that the threat of execution does not deter real murderers. U.S. states that use the death penalty do not, on average, have lower murder rates than states that don't; some actually have higher rates, though it could be argued that they would have had higher rates anyway. Hard to know. How else could you think of this whole issue?

- The average age at first sexual intercourse is under 16 years for U.S. teens, the lowest age of any major industrialized country. It seems a bit young. (Is it? Why?) Meanwhile, the United States also has a much higher teen pregnancy rate than most other industrialized nations and a vastly higher sexually transmitted disease (STD) rate, in part because we do such a bad job at sex education. (Sure, you can teach abstinence, but the majority of young people who nonetheless choose to be sexually active consequently don't get decent information on contraception, STD prevention, or for that matter sexual relationships in general.) Any ways to change our angle here? (Hint: why does "sexually active" have to mean exactly *one* form of sexual activity? Isn't that just a bit, well, unimaginative?)

- Consider the "performance-enhancing drugs" used, and abused, by some athletes. High school and even younger athletes risk their health for an unnatural edge; meanwhile, on a global scale, the World Anti-Doping Agency (great name, huh?) polices competitions such as the Olympics. Other competitors want to stay drug-free but also to compete on a level playing field. Any other ways to approach all of this?

- Especially in rough economic times, large numbers of people fall into poverty and need some kind of help, at least for a short time. On the other hand, dependency and abuse are worries in the welfare system as we have known it. How else might welfare systems be organized? (One hint: compare welfare practices around the world.) We also struggle with how to respond, person to person, to people asking for money in the streets. We want to help, we say, but have also learned to wonder what the money is really going for. Some of us give a dollar anyway—how can you turn away? Others make it a policy to refuse. Couldn't there be some rather different ways of meeting the situation. (Hint: what if what's given isn't money?)

- People who disagree profoundly with important political and social decisions need some way to visibly register their disagreement and attempt to sway others to their point of view—in short, to protest. But what is the best form for such protest? Too many of the current forms of protest are so obviously pushed into invisibility or irrelevance that the protestors become embittered and cynical—or turn to violence. (Witness the fringes of the antiabortion and antilogging movements, just for two examples.) See if you can imagine healthier and more productive forms of protest. What would be two steps toward making them workable?

3. Problem-solving strategies address, of course, problems. But creativity can go farther still. Why wait until something becomes a problem before trying to make creative improvements? Everything can be creatively improved all the time. We can go beyond even prevention. Ultimately, the most proactive strategy of all is to try to creatively reimagine the world in every way we can.

Look around, then, for institutions or practices that are *not* currently ethical problems, and consider how you might creatively improve them in ethical directions.

One example: we now have Mother's Day, Father's Day, and increasingly Grandparents' Day, but mostly as occasions for sending a card or maybe going on a shopping trip. How can we better celebrate each other—more fully, more meaningfully, more consistently? Fun question, eh? Also, by the way, what about *Children's Day?* Cat Day? School or State Day? Who/what else are we not celebrating enough?

Or again, might we soon need to develop a new kind of etiquette for e-mail, cell phones, etc., so that we are not constantly "on call," expected to respond just as fast as the messages arrive, and, too often, only half attentive to wherever we actually are and whoever we are actually with? Better start now. (And a hint: must an "etiquette" of this sort be merely a set of *constraints?*)

A variation: look for places where ethics has been notably *successful*, and then ask whether the same successes can be generalized to other areas. Find solutions first, so to speak, and then search for new problems. Chapter 1 spoke of solidarity, for example, as when families or neighborhoods shave their own heads to support people who have lost their hair to chemotherapy. We have the general idea. But are there other and still more powerful ways, both practical and symbolic, to show solidarity with those fighting cancer or similar diseases? With the dying? With children? With soldiers? With each other, day to day? With the Earth?

While you're at it, why not invent some new ethical practices out of the blue? Create something completely new!

5

CONFLICTS AS CREATIVE
OPPORTUNITIES

Here's a debate for you.

A: Humans have always eaten meat! You vegetarians want to go against nature.

B: You think people have always lined up at McDonald's for their quarter-pounder with shake and fries?

A: So what do you want? Some juice bar with a little organic carrot and spring water? Give me a break! Besides, you animal-rights fanatics want to stop all medical research. What about the cures for so many diseases, found through experiments on animals? If it weren't for those experiments, you wouldn't even be here to bad-mouth them.

B: Why do we need all those new cosmetics and toilet-bowl cleaners? That's what 99% of animal testing is about! You're just rationalizing torture.

The topic is a vital one. There are possibilities in it, some of them even hinted at in this little exchange. But the discussion itself immediately degenerates into combat. Everything is sarcasm and accusation and stereotype ("you animal-rights fanatics," etc.). Differences are exaggerated—indeed, just assumed. They *tell* each other rather than *ask* each other what they think. No options are considered except the most extreme and ridiculous.

Sure it's familiar. Sure it's disheartening. But does disagreement really block any possibility for creative conflict resolution? Does conflict make dialogue impossible? Why couldn't conflict be productive—even, believe it or not, *creative*?

LOOK FOR OPENINGS

You now have the resources to approach ethical debates in a different spirit. You already have a set of methods for finding "provocations" in a variety of settings. You understand the reasons: inviting exotic associations, watching for suggestive facts, revisiting outlying parts of the problem, etc., are ways of changing your angle, looking at things from new perspectives, thinking out of the box. So could we not take conflict—disagreement, unusual (to you) perspectives, even if angrily argued—in the same spirit?

Sometimes there are creative openings right in front of us. For example, in the exchange above, both A and B ask a lot of questions. (Go back and look.) True, many of them are sarcastic. We could still take them as real questions. Some of them are perfectly practical questions, too. Why *do* we need all those new cosmetics and toilet-bowl cleaners? And what *do* vegetarians want in place of McDonald's?

Right here in plain view in the middle of this little food fight, then, we already have a way to turn in a different direction. Try answering some of those questions. Follow up that last one a little, maybe. What *do* vegetarians want? A vegetarian fast-food chain? What might be its trademark dish? There are all sorts of interesting possibilities and even business opportunities here.

Or again, what *is* a natural diet for humans? "Humans have always eaten meat," maybe; but B is probably right that it wouldn't have been anything like current amounts: more like small amounts very occasionally. Hmm . . . and what would *that* look like in modern terms? A Japanese diet, maybe?

Now try to widen these openings, to turn the debate explicitly into more of a creative exploration, even (yes) a kind of brainstorm. You are B, maybe, back at the beginning of the above debate. A has made her point, for better or worse. You could blast right back, sarcastically too, like in the original, which has the predictable effect of making A talk even more like a battering ram. Then again, you could try something else.

B: I suppose you're right that humans have always eaten some meat. But for most people, most of the time, meat would have been rare, the exception and not the rule. Eating meat McDonald's-style, anyway, is not the norm.

To be very clear: this kind of approach is not just more civil. The key thing is that it also opens up some creative space where none seemed to exist before. Glimpses of a middle way—for example, a *low-meat* diet. Already, then, right here at the beginning, you move the discussion onto a more productive path.

In the original, A ridicules B's response, bringing up an alternative (spring water and carrot, anyone?) that B pretty clearly does not favor, and then changes the subject with another wild accusation. Let's try again.

> **A** (taking care this time):   I'm pretty sure our ancestors ate meat whenever they could get it, though you might be right that it wasn't very often. But I'm interested in what you propose instead. Eating no meat at all, ever?

This time A acknowledges B's statement in turn, while still disagreeing with it, and then, instead of assuming that she knows what kind of alternative B actually favors, she does something unheard of—she *asks*. And now they can talk recipes. It turns out that many people are quite curious about vegetarian diets. Just finding out about them makes a useful conversation right there.

Sometimes you may end up in a debate where the other participants really do just want to have a fight. You can only play along, or opt out. But it may also be that people (anyway, most people) engage in ethical debates in this way only because they have no live example of what else an ethical discussion could be. In that case, you may be able to change the course and outcome of the discussion just by the way in which you yourself talk. Your most powerful tool will be a single-minded focus on unfolding new possibilities in the ideas that come up.

And notice: it's not merely that a brainstorming approach is more likely to yield productive results. Since the creativity here is essentially the whole group's, brainstorming also requires that we listen to and value all of the participants. It is also, in short, more *ethical!*

SEEK COMMON GROUND

Still more is possible in approaching many ethical debates. We can learn to seek out and work from areas of agreement, from *common ground.*

We learn to approach ethical issues expecting conflict and sharp disagreement. Maybe it's partly because of the media: conflict is always more dramatic, seemingly more interesting. Anyway, we certainly hear about conflict all the time—much less often about the background agreements that in fact frame our lives and even our areas of conflict—and so much so that we absorb the implicit message that conflict really is the basic reality, the "given," of our ethical lives together. We are often even trained to look for the conflicts and to sharpen them into clear oppositions—that's one source of "dilemma-ism," in fact.

To reapproach ethical debates with a creative agenda, we need to look in the other direction: toward *shared values.* And, believe it or not, they are there to be found.

Take the animal issue again. Few people really want to cause unnecessary pain and suffering to other animals (right?). People who eat meat or support drug tests on other animals would at least favor trying to treat the animals in a humane way, which would already be major progress, actually. So why not start there, on common ground? We can ask, "How is more humane use of animals possible? What would be two new creative steps in that direction? And where it really isn't possible, isn't there at least sometimes a case for letting the animals off?"

On the other hand, we do not want to cause unnecessary pain and suffering to ourselves, either. This is why vegetarians and opponents of animal testing need to argue that vegetarian diets are actually healthier (certainly adequate) and that animal testing is often unhelpful. But always? Again we are invited to explore a range of options against a background of, well, largely shared values. The real argument lies in the realm of facts and alternatives—and, again, it is open to some creative rethinking.

Or take the debate over same-sex marriage, another wide-ranging debate that touches deep nerves. Some same-sex couples and their supporters absolutely insist on the right to share in marriage. Some conservatives and others cannot even begin to imagine such a thing. All the same, once again, the debate is framed by some striking but seldom noticed agreements. Especially this: *both sides believe in marriage.* The debate is not about whether marriage itself is a good thing. It is only because same-sex advocates care about marriage so much that they argue, so passionately and persistently, that same-sex couples ought to be able to share it.

So is this glass half empty or half full? You can focus on the areas of disagreement and say "half empty." But you could as readily focus on their broad background agreement and say "half full." The rather amazing fact, right in front of us and yet totally invisible if we concentrate just on the areas of conflict, is that the "opposed" sides have common ground. The issue comes up only because they both care deeply about the same thing.

I don't mean that the minute you find some common ground you have somehow resolved the issue. No. What you *do* find, again, is a basis for shared problem-solving, for genuine brainstorming. As Roger Fisher and William Ury say in their influential book *Getting to Yes*, it's not the other side that's really the problem: it's the *problem* that's the problem.

Rather than fighting each other, you can now stand on the same side, even with your differences, and take up the shared creative challenge together.

Maybe what we need is a legal structure allowing for different kinds of marriage. I've already mentioned that countries like France and some U.S. states are establishing civil unions as alternatives for marriage-like commitments (for both same-sex and opposite-sex couples) and that some conservatives are promoting a sort of super-marriage, called "covenant marriage." Marriage is already diversifying. Others—mostly conservatives too, surprisingly enough—have argued that the government should get out of the business of making marriage law entirely and allow religious and other communities to unite people however they see fit.

So maybe there are ways to improve committed relationships, of all sorts, for *everyone*. Wouldn't that be a worthy and absolutely shareable goal? Why not work on it together?

AND WHERE WE DISAGREE . . .

Sometimes, of course, we actively disagree all the way down. Even so, though, it turns out that a little creative thinking can take us a long way.

Take the debate about meat-eating one last time. Certainly there are moral concerns about meat-eating. But the fact is that not everyone shares those concerns, even after a lot of argument. In the meantime, though, many people now eat low-meat or no-meat diets for other reasons: personal health, maybe, or for the sake of the environment. Those moving away from meat, then, could make common cause. Don't insist that you must also share a whole moral philosophy. You don't disagree about *diet*, only about (some of) the underlying reasons.

In fact, even when interests are radically opposed, we can still find unexpected solutions that bring the two sides together.

Think about the rise of whale watching. For decades, moral and political pressure mounted to stop whale hunting, but the whale industry, from the shipowners to the crews, resisted. No surprise—their livelihood was at stake. Others became resolutely opposed to the whalers. Members of Greenpeace began to motor out in small boats in the open ocean to place themselves between the harpooners and the whales. No common ground, right?

Maybe not. Yet about a decade ago a transformation occurred. Shipowners began to realize that they could make far more money taking people out to *watch* whales than they could by killing them. Suddenly everything looked different. Now the old whale ports have become whale-watching ports, and we are discovering that even the supposedly most hostile whales (and why wouldn't they be hostile after three centuries of being hunted without mercy?) can be affectionate and curious. People are even out there making music with them.

Did the whalers change their minds about whales? Some did, I'm sure, once they were freed to look at whales another way. But many did not. They may still look at whales as a source of jobs and income. Yet, even so, there turns out to be a better way to make money from them than killing them—and a way that makes peace with the whales' defenders after all.

We've learned to call this sort of outcome a "win–win" solution. Fisher and Ury call it "dove-tailing" values. You've seen fine wood boxes or furniture with interlocked wedge-shaped cuts (like a dove's tail) that fit together to form a tight joint. Likewise with values. Genuinely *different* values can still be *compatible.* With a little creativity we can speak to both (to all) at once.

FOR PRACTICE 𝕊

1. Read the exchanges below in the tone of voice you'd normally expect in such debates. Notice where and how they degenerate. Then revisit them as invitations to creative problem-solving. What possibilities do you see in them? If you found yourself in the midst of one of these debates, how could you move it in a constructive direction? After you have worked through these, look in the same spirit at the letters to the editor in your local paper or the exchanges of comments on controversial issues on interactive weblogs.

Rich and Poor

T: I can't believe the insensitivity of some people. Everywhere there is hunger and need. Twenty thousand children in this world die every day of starvation or diseases that are easy to prevent. Yet we waste and waste and waste.

M: Yeah, but the poor will always be with us. You're ranting and raving about how terrible we are, but if you think about it, the poor in America are rich compared to even the rich in other countries. Whole families in Africa get less money in a year than one welfare mother in Chicago gets in a month.

T: Oh, right, I'd like to see you try to live on it, even for a week.

M: I certainly wouldn't sit around all day feeling sorry for myself. I believe in work—that's how to get ahead in America. As my grandfather used to say, if you need a hand, look at the end of your arm. God helps those who help themselves.

T: A really sensible God would help those who need help!

Sex Education

A: Do you know that so-called "abstinence" sex education curricula only mention contraceptives in order to tell kids that they don't work? And this is the twenty-first century! First of all, it's just not true. No method is perfect, but the best methods are 95 to 99% effective.

B: That's not the point. Set them up with contraception and what will they do—have sex.

C: Next you'll want mandatory chastity belts.

B: Not a bad idea.

A: They'll have sex, many of them, whether you "set them up" with contraception or not. So if the schools are not telling them anything about contraception except the lie that it doesn't work, of course they won't use it. That's why teen pregnancy rates are going up again.

B: No, it's because we have an oversexed society. Where are we going to start to change that if not in the schools?

Speeders

P: We take speeding way too lightly. Speeding is an amazing form of carelessness with other people's lives and bodies. It's really a form of assault with a deadly weapon.

Q: In some Islamic countries you can be executed for speeding.

R: That's a little extreme, isn't it?

S: The dangerous ones are the kids who weave in and out of traffic, ten or twenty miles per hour faster than everyone else. But no more than the geezer doing 45 in the left-hand lane. Anyway, it's all part of the scene on the roads: annoying, maybe, but not exactly a capital offense. You guys need to take a few days off or something.

P: I want more cops. And sure, they can ticket the people going too slow, too. But we have to do something, don't we? You can't exactly put a big flashing sign on people's cars saying "Look out! I'm a speeder!"

S: Some places don't even have a speed limit, you know.

Q: Why do we make cars that can go 120, anyway?

Business Ethics

W: I don't think the big corporate CEOs would be polluting the air and water around their factories if they were breathing and drinking it too. They should be expected to live right there.

X: They're not out to hurt people. Some of them care very much about the environment.

W: I'm sure that some do. The problem is that they don't see the connection between what they do and its effects—because the effects are somewhere else. *Their* air is still clean. They need to think of the local people, whose lives and families are being affected.

X: Maybe the local people choose to live with less clean air or water because it's cheaper, or they don't really care. You don't have to clean up their air for them.

Y: You know, you could generalize W's idea. What if the executives of companies that make shoddy drugs or dangerous cars had to use them too? Boy, would standards improve!

Z: Don't consumers have any responsibility for what they buy? People use cigarettes knowing perfectly well that they are cancer sticks. What are you going to do, require the tobacco company CEOs to be chain-smokers?

X: Hey, don't forget the actual workers. Better force them to chain-smoke too.

2. For each of the "hot button" issues outlined below, ask what are the points of agreement, or at least the points of potentially compatible values, between the two familiar contending sides. Look for the half-full glass rather than the half-empty one. List your results. Then ask whether any new ideas emerge from your exploration.

Example: *capital punishment*. Shared or compatible values might include:

- *Life* (strong for both sides: both insist that life is precious, which is why murder is considered by both so heinous a crime, why the pro side thinks murderers deserve death and why the anti side thinks that execution only doubles the crime).

• *Appropriate punishment* (since both sides condemn murder, both propose "ultimate punishments" in some sense: execution or life in prison).

• *Deterrence* (preventing future murders).

• *Fairness* (convictions must be fair; the execution of innocent people and racially tainted verdicts are wrong).

Now ask, "Does this list suggest new approaches to punishment?" Some options might include:

• *Third ways,* besides either execution *or* life in prison. (Could convicted murderers offer their lives for some kind of good? Dangerous but necessary jobs?)

• *Prevention.* (We do understand something about what drives people to kill other people: everything from emotional and social stresses—unemployment, for example—to the easy availability of weapons. Anything proactive to be done here?)

• *Restorative work* in communities damaged by crime. (Check out the "restorative justice" movement.)

And what else? (Your turn . . .)

Here are some issues for you.

• *Meat-eating and animal testing.* This chapter introduces these questions, but you can take them much farther.

• *Drugs.* (Hint: take some time here to define your terms, especially "drug" itself, before considering the relevant values.)

• *Affirmative action.* (Ditto.)

• *Welfare.* (That is, how should society respond to the needs of the down-and-out?)

Check out any newspaper for many more.

6

THREE TOUGH QUESTIONS

So far, I have said very little about some of the most controversial and painful issues in ethics, abortion in particular. Also,
I have not said anything about certain pressing but confusing
ethical issues like environmental ethics. This is on purpose—I
have been saving them for the end.

Now is their time. What about a little creative problem-
solving even on these most difficult of issues? Isn't it worth a
try? And maybe, just maybe, the results could be far more dramatic than we expect.

ABORTION

Most readers, I am sure, know the outlines of the abortion
debate all too well, especially when it is reduced to shouting
"Life!" on the one side and "Choice!" on the other. We might

as well begin right there. In the spirit of the last chapter, we might start right off with a surprising but still fairly obvious observation. As general values, at least, life and choice are not incompatible. In fact, all of us value both.

Every one of us is pro-life. Life is what makes love and community and beauty and everything else possible. Those acts associated with creating and preserving and honoring life—sex, childbirth, nurturing a baby, caring for the sick, mourning the dead—are among the deepest and most profound of life's experiences.

Every one of us is also pro-choice. Freedom, self-determination, the right to control what happens to our own bodies—this is absolutely basic too. In politics, in the stores, in lifestyle —choice is everything. Some people even think that seat belts and speed limits are unjustified limits on physical freedom, but these are trivial restrictions compared to pregnancy and childbirth.

In short, we have *two* sets of basic values here, not just one "right" one. And the question can only be how to relate or balance them in tough cases. So even the abortion debate could, conceivably, be more of a collaboration than a fight.

I know, I know, the idea takes some getting used to. It might help to hear that many people are already working from common ground, or at least compatible values, in the debate. When the welfare laws were up for revision in 1996, for example, some legislators proposed denying assistance to children born of mothers under 18 or currently on welfare or children whose paternity hadn't been established. In response a remarkable thing happened. Nearly all major organizations on *both* sides of the abortion issue came out against the proposal, including the National Right to Life Committee, Planned Parenthood, the U.S. Catholic Conference, and the National Organization of Women. Both sides feared that the results would be to coerce abortions among poor women. Both sides made the connections back to economic conditions. In fact, pro-choice and pro-life organizations jointly designed a comprehensive child-support reform plan.

Common ground emerged—in face of a common threat. But why wait for that? Indeed, some people haven't. From 1993–2000 a worldwide organization called Search for Common Ground sponsored a dialogue project specifically on the abortion issue, called The Common Ground Network for Life and Choice—again: Life *and* Choice—devoted to constructive listening and working from a common agenda. The Network spread quickly across the entire country. Lately even some politicians seem to be moving toward somewhat more constructive problem-solving.

If a problem seems insoluble and deeply divisive, remember, it's a good idea to try to head it off in the first place. Here, then, let us ask—together—how we can reduce the demand for abortions themselves. Is there any realistic way to reduce the number of unwanted pregnancies and/or to keep those unintended pregnancies that do occur from being unwanted?

More than half of all women who seek abortion were not using contraception when they got pregnant. Why? We need to find out. Lack of access? Lack of education? Violence? These things can be changed. Changing them might not even be controversial.

And what about the other half, women who used contraception and still got pregnant? Again, we need to find out why. Poor or difficult-to-use methods? Resistance from spouses and lovers? These things, too, can be changed. With a fraction of the energy and intensity put into the present abortion debate, they *could* be changed.

Why does abortion sometimes become so desperate a need? Why would a child, another child, or a child at the "wrong" time, sometimes be a disaster for a mother or family? What can be done about that?

One answer is that women still confront inflexible expectations about career tracks, work schedules, and schooling. Again, this is a fixable problem. We need more flexible expectations and alternative work and schooling patterns that do not punish or impede women (and men) who also choose major family responsibilities. Most European countries are far ahead of the United States in this area (another useful contrast). It's not so hard to work out the details.

Equal pay for women is, or ought to be, our goal. Shared childraising has everything to recommend it. At the very least, fathers should be expected to support their children financially (at present, even with greatly expanded enforcement, only a third contribute anything at all). Paid parental leaves are the norm in Europe. My students, working on this problem in a creative mode, have suggested still other ideas, such as a system of "adoptive grandparents." What do you think?

One of my ethics classes was discussing the abortion issue with our college chaplain. He remarked that in his decade or so at the college he had seen only three or four students carry pregnancies to term and stay in school too. A (male) student later wrote the following:

> I'm pro-life, but I can't really blame a fellow student for getting an abortion when the alternative is leaving college. Your whole future is at stake. I think the real question is: why should she be put in that position?

Why, indeed? So the question to us is, "What can we change—teachers, students, chaplains—so that fewer women are put in this position in the future?" Class schedules, assignments, how financial aid is calculated? How hard would that be?

It sounds like a broad shared agenda after all. This is where we could put our energies for an actual resolution, instead of just another few rounds of the usual fight. Why not?

MORE ON ABORTION

All of this is still only a beginning in thinking creatively about the abortion issue. Mostly you have to take it from here yourself. I want to briefly offer just one more idea, this time to provoke some creative thinking of a rather different sort.

The abortion issue is so persistent and so painful partly because it involves certain losses, indeed tragic losses, no matter what is chosen or how you look at it. Different lives and life choices are at stake, all of them precious, and they cannot all be lived out.

The most obvious loss, of course, is the physical life of the fetus, the child-to-be. The loss of a pregnancy to miscarriage is acknowledged all around as a serious loss. Why not the same in abortion? The usual response is that sometimes the other stakes—the life prospects of the pregnant woman and/or those around her—are also great, though less visible. Often, surely, this is true. In practice, though, we have trouble holding both kinds of stakes, or potential losses, in mind at the same time. Tragic choices trouble us—we like to see the world in black and white—so there is a tendency (on *both* sides) to discount or even deny the losses on the other side.

But why? Mightn't this kind of denial even be part of the problem? Trying another tack, suppose that we consider how to make the loss of the fetus—the loss of a potential life—both more visible and at the same time possibly more bearable. Japanese Buddhists, I understand, have developed a kind of memorial ritual, even sometimes a kind of apology, for aborted as well as miscarried fetuses (also, strikingly, for animals deliberately killed in the course of drug experiments).

Mizuko Kuyo, it is called. It is a way of facing rather than denying the consequences—underscoring the seriousness of the choice, which is surely good from the point of view of *all* sides—but also reaching some kind of closure, making it possible to go on. Loss can be acknowledged without shutting down the hard choices required. Those facing such a choice can have a better way to get a grip on just what is at stake. Those who have made such choices can have a better way to make peace with them. What if we develop such a ritual too?

Again, this is only a starting point—a little brainstorm starting with "compare and contrast." The idea is sketchy and needs development. But that is just the point. Don't immediately start seeing possible problems. Ask how it *might* work for us, rather than declaring that it can't and therefore leaving things just as they are. Even on this issue, as "stuck" and polarized as it usually seems, so much more is possible.

ASSISTED SUICIDE

Many people would say that suicide could be a moral choice in some extreme circumstances. Choosing death might be better than living in extreme pain or disability or despair.

Some people go a step farther to argue that people can legitimately request *help* in dying if, for reasons of disability or other incapacity (for example, being legally prohibited from getting the necessary drugs themselves), they are not able effectively to take their own lives. Naturally doctors would be the ones asked to help. Thus we come to the issue of physician-assisted suicide, or PAS for short—a second tough question.

A recent and very visible proponent of PAS was Dr. Jack Kevorkian, a physician who publicly assisted suicides using a lethal-injection device he had invented. To some, Kevorkian was a humanitarian crusader for the right to die. To others, his work was ghoulish and shameful. Kevorkian was finally jailed after he sent a videotape of an assisted death to a Michigan TV station and it was shown on nationwide TV. PAS has been legalized, though, in the state of Oregon (it is also legal in some European countries) and, in fact, may be gaining more acceptance in Kevorkian's absence than he himself was able to win for it. At the same time, it has inspired a devoted "pro-life" opposition.

Pulling out our problem-solving toolbox, we could start by asking, "Mightn't there be a way to achieve some of the same ends as PAS but without its ethical liabilities?" That is, is there a way to allow people some dignified way to choose death in special circumstances, when they cannot act on their own, without making death too easy a choice or compromising doctors' commitment to life?

How about this: doctors might not offer such aid, but special new professionals, trained in both medicine and psychology, could. Think of it as an extension of, say, hospice care. We already understand that the dying need special kinds of care and empowerment, and not necessarily the kinds with which the rest of medicine is concerned.

Again, here are people willing and sometimes even eager to die and surely preferring to die without a lingering sense of controversy and dishonor hanging over their heads. Remembering that sometimes "the problem is the opportunity," we need to ask, "Could this wish be an opportunity for something?" For what?

How about this: could there not be alternative ways to die—maybe on heroic but dangerous or one-way missions? Or medical experiments? We might even create a new language, new rituals, even new kinds of public recognition and honor for people willing to go out in this way.

Once again, too, it would be useful to ask the preventive and background questions that may allow us to reframe "the" issue in much different terms. For one thing, why do some people find death so appealing a choice in the first place? Really, why?

Pain is one reason: intense, relentless pain that the sufferer knows will not end until death. Of course you'd want to die as soon as possible if you are dying in such pain anyway.

This suggests, surely, a major effort to develop better painkillers. It also suggests rethinking how we limit certain drugs. Doctors are trained not to prescribe extremely strong painkillers because they readily become addictive. Thus, for a time, most doctors wouldn't give morphine to dying patients, even though they were dying and addiction would hardly matter! There's also some resistance to certain pain-relieving drugs because some of them are not legal—marijuana and heroin, for example—though both are widely used in other countries for pain relief in some kinds of terminal conditions. Probably it's time to rethink this too.

We tend to assume that extreme pain is the main or only reason some people seek PAS. Surveys suggest, however, that the actual reasons are often different. People report feeling helpless, useless, and abandoned. As Chapter 2 mentions, some of my students once found a website that included biographies of the people that Kevorkian had helped to die. Though it was a pro-Kevorkian website, we began to realize that Kevorkian became a last resort for many people because they not only were in pain but also lacked any kind of family or social support. In some cases, their spouses or children were driven away by their very condition.

Here the right answer is surely not death. It is to create communities of care such that no one is abandoned in this way. And once again, that's a challenge to all of us, too—not just to stand by and judge the morality of certain kinds of suicide but to keep people from the kinds of loss that drive them to such desperation in the first place.

Sometimes, still, there are cases when pain is so intense and hope so remote that it seems hard to deny that death can be a considered and humane choice. Your heart goes out to people in this situation, and I know that if I were one of them, I might well wish the same thing.

We could try a little creative compromise here. Many people on both sides would be willing to accept a policy that allowed PAS under tightly controlled conditions. Several independent doctors would have to concur. Waiting periods could be required. Double-checks would be necessary to be sure patients were not just temporarily depressed. Communities and governments would need to be sure that people in pain always have alternatives. Then, though, given all of this, if a person resolutely seeks to die, isn't it time to respect their wishes?

It may be possible, in short, to legalize assisted suicide in a limited way that both acknowledges the concerns of the current opponents (fears of free-lance "Doctor Deaths," like Kevorkian; concerns that it will become an "easy way out") and recognizes that, sometimes at least, it can be a humane and proper choice. It's not too hard to figure this out.

Just this kind of solution has been adopted in the state of Oregon (and recently reaffirmed by 60% of the voters), by the way, with results that, while still controversial, at least don't sound like an epidemic of suicides. Only about one hundred people have legally requested doctors' help in dying since 1998. Surely we can be glad that more people haven't asked *and* that PAS was there for those who did.

ENVIRONMENTAL ETHICS

We know that we face an environmental crisis: air and water and land pollution, shrinking resources, global warming, species extinctions. We know that we need to massively recycle, live more lightly, pay more attention to the natural world.

There are creative and ingenious ways to make some of these changes. Hybrid cars already get over seventy miles per gallon of gas just by such simple innovations as not running the motor when the car is stopped and using braking energy to recharge the batteries. Whale-watching boat trips and rain forest "eco-tourism" are building a viable, long-term economy based on preserving and indeed *treasuring* nature.

Examples like these already teach an important lesson. Though environmental values are sometimes defined as "special interests" in opposition to economic values or other sorts of interests, there is in fact a great deal of common ground. Even in purely economic terms, most environmental measures are actually more profitable than one-shot destruction, which enriches a few investors but leaves the community far poorer, indeed often wrecked and displaced (think of clear-cutting or rain forest burning). Economies farther into solar and wind power have fuller employment and healthier populations than those more invested in oil and nuclear power—far better even in the (very limited) economic terms to which well-being is too often reduced.

Besides, when we speak of the Earth, we are speaking of the air and the water and the living communities of land and sea upon which all of us, all of our children and our children's children, and all of the other creatures depend. These are hardly "special" interests—they are universal, common, basic interests, which literally "ground" all others.

Still, I believe that the question of environmental ethics differs from the more established debates over abortion or PAS. Here it is not really that we have two sets of well-defined values in polar opposition. It's more that we really don't yet know what or how to think about environmental values at all. They're too new, too unfamiliar, too long-term, too *big*.

Moreover, they are often, as yet, too negative. My students—like you, maybe?—are both increasingly well-informed about environmental threats and also more and more pessimistic. Nature is still pictured mainly as a source of problems and dangers, and environmental ethics is therefore reduced to an insistence on limits and caution. And true enough, limits and caution would be a good idea. But we need more than that. We are talking about the *Earth* here. We need some *inspiration*: some fascination, some sense of possibility, a sense for how transformed a relation to the larger-than-human world could be.

There's a good creative challenge. Much is already happening to meet it, too. Established religions are coming to the forefront of environmentalism as they insist on honoring the Earth as God's creation. People are founding "eco-steries" on the model of the medieval world's monasteries, places where nature is honored and preserved "for the long haul" and for its own sake. NASA is experimenting with living arks, realizing that entire living communities must go into space if long missions are to be possible at all. Some people are developing an ethic of respect for other animals; other people are developing new forms of life that actively embody such a respect—some absolutely new and fascinating, like musicians creating new musical forms with orcas.

Now it's our turn. Are there more creative possibilities still?

What if—just for one quick provocation—we deliberately reverse the negativism of so much contemporary environmentalism and imagine instead a *celebratory* environmentalism? Suppose, for instance, that we create new environmental holidays? Festivals, maybe, for bird migrations and eclipses. Already at New Year's many people all across the country venture out, before dawn, to count birds for the Audubon Society.

Why not take this much farther? Imagine weeks of preparation by eager schoolchildren learning to identify birds. Imagine the hopefulness of the observers that a rare bird might come their way, like amateur astronomers hoping to discover a comet.

Speaking of comets, we could also imagine "star nights," on which all lights everywhere are turned out, even in the blazing cities, timed to coincide with meteor showers, eclipses, occlusions. At the beginning of his essay "Nature," Ralph Waldo Emerson wrote "If the stars came out only one night in a thousand years, how people would believe and adore, and preserve from generation to generation, remembrance of the miracle they'd been shown." For us, the miracle is there every dark and clear night—we just need a little help to see it.

The word "holiday" itself, by the way, comes from "holy day," a time when we remember what really matters. Who wouldn't want a few new ones? And when we come to the Earth as a holy place, in love and joy rather than (mainly) in fear, treasuring and preserving it isn't even a question.

Finally, we could take a new look at the *old* holidays too, for most of these are rooted in natural cycles as well. Winter Solstice, the moment when the long descent of the cold and the dark finally ends, the days stop shortening, the sun begins its reascent. It is the rebirth of the year, and of course at the moment of greatest darkness we celebrate with lights, on Christmas trees and in menorahs (Hanukah) and kinaras (Kwanzaa). Spring brings the Vernal Equinox: the Earth itself is, well, resurrected, bursting into new life. Ancient Samhain, midway between Fall Equinox and Winter Solstice, became All Saints' Day—its eve, All Hallows' Eve, which we now call Halloween, the death festival, as the leaves fall and the darkness descends. No light without dark, no life without death.

It is in places like this that creativity has its greatest play in ethics. Yes, we can find new solutions and transform even the most stuck and familiar debate. That is the project to which most of this book has invited you. Here, though, the invitation is also to help recreate and expand our ethics, our values, themselves. Big, necessary, good work.

FOR PRACTICE &

This book is now at an end. It is up to you to make the practice of creativity your own. I hope you are inspired to jump right in. Pick up a newspaper for starters, check out the ethical issues that are arising—today, tomorrow, next week— and begin to work on them. Most of the "For Practice" parts of this book have also listed a variety of issues, often with hints about some creative ways to reframe them. Revisit them now. Carry your creative rethinking still farther.

Don't demand of yourself that you arrive at a definitive solution right away. Just carefully put the tools in this book into use. Learn all you can about the issues. Brainstorm, alone and with friends. Go to "extremes." Think preventively; look for common ground and compatible values and the opportunities even in the worst problems.

Remember that the invitation, from the point of view of creative problem-solving, is not mainly to find more effective ways of promoting your own ethical point of view. That is what most people will expect, perhaps. But your angle is different. You are looking to *transform* or *reframe* the whole issue, rather than to justify one point of view over others on the ethical issues. You are not acting for one side or the other so much as for the community as a whole, for all of us.

Make something of your results. You may decide to change your own behavior, for starters—to embody creative ethical solutions in your life and/or to make of your own life more of a creative inspiration to others. Talk to people: family, friends, students or teachers, coworkers and colleagues, elected officials. Write letters to the newspaper or guest editorials. Join community discussion groups. Play up the creative and constructive aspect: make suggestions, rather than complaining or criticizing. Some students have even secured an hour once a week on the college radio station and run a Creative Problem-Solving Call-In Hour. (*That's* putting it on the line!) Go to meetings of your City Council or County Planning Commission (or PTA, Neighborhood Association, Precinct . . .). Probably you'll be surprised at how few other people show up. Just one person willing to speak up can make a real difference. Get some new ideas into circulation.

Much of this is just good citizenship with a creative ethical angle. Yet don't underestimate the power of creative thinking to *inspire* people. It's not very often that elected officials or moral leaders, say, hear from people with creative, out-of-the-box ideas. It's easier to just gripe or advocate some prepackaged moral position —or never get in touch at all. Someone whose attitude is more creative and constructive—that is, *you*—will stand out. Go do it.

NOTES AND SOURCES

FOR FURTHER READING

Extended introductions to creative thinking are Edward de Bono, *Serious Creativity* (HarperCollins, 1992) and *Lateral Thinking* (Harper, 1970); Barry Nalebuff and Ian Ayres, *Why Not? How to Use Everyday Ingenuity to Solve Problems Big and Small* (Harvard Business School Press, 2003); Charlie and Maria Girsch, *Inventivity* (Creativity Central, 1999); and Marvin Levine, *Effective Problem Solving* (Prentice Hall, second edition, 1993). On proactive thinking, Stephen Covey's *The Seven Habits of Highly Effective People* (Simon and Schuster, 1990) is classic.

Check out this book's twin, too: *Creativity for Critical Thinkers* (Oxford University Press, 2007). Most of the methods and themes are similar, but you will find there a range of very different examples, differently developed.

I also have written two other textbooks in ethics. *A Practical Companion to Ethics* (Oxford University Press, third edition, 2005) is a discussion of about the same length but much more inclusive: it is a survey of a variety of skills that help "make ethics work," including creativity but other skills as well. My other ethics book, *A 21st Century Ethical Toolbox* (Oxford University Press, 2001, second edition forthcoming), is a full-length treatment of all of the themes only sketched in *A Practical Companion to Ethics*, as well as a treatment of values and ethical theories and a number of applied topics. It is designed to be the main text for a college ethics course. Check out the *Toolbox* if you want to explore how the skills in this book take their place within a comprehensive approach to ethics as a whole. The aim of *Creative Problem-Solving in Ethics* is to offer a fuller and more single-minded treatment specifically of ethical creativity.

SOURCES

Chapter 1: The Heinz dilemma is cited from Lawrence Kohlberg, "Stage and Sequence: The Cognitive-Developmental Approach to Socialization," in D. A. Goslin, ed., *Handbook of Socialization Theory and Research* (Rand McNally, 1969), p. 379. For "Good Morning, Children," I am indebted to Benjamin and Rosamund Zander's lovely book *The Art of Possibility* (Harvard Business School Press, 2000), p. 164.

Chapter 2: The extended description of the Schiavo case is my abridgement and adaptation of an entry from Wikipedia (http://en.wikipedia.org/wiki/Schiavo, accessed 7/7/05).

Chapter 3: On the exotic-association (random-word) method and some of the other methods introduced in this chapter, see the works of Edward de Bono cited above. The closing dilemma is cited from Jean-Paul Sartre, *Existentialism and Human Emotions* (Philosophical Library, 1957), pp. 24–25.

Chapter 4: On pornography, David Steinberg is quoted from his essay "The Roots of Pornography," in Michael Kimmel, ed., *Men Confront Pornography* (Meridian, 1990), p. 58.

Chapter 5: On the origins of brainstorming, see Alex Osborne's *Applied Imagination: Principles and Procedures of Creative Problem-Solving* (Creative Education Foundation, 1993). *A 21st Century Ethical Toolbox* offers more on conflicts as creative opportunities. Roger Fisher's and William Ury's classic book is *Getting to*

Yes (Penguin, 1983). See also Tom Rusk, *The Power of Ethical Persuasion* (Penguin, 1993).

Chapter 6: Search for Common Ground can be found on the web at www.searchforcommonground.org; for the Network for Life and Choice project, see http://www.sfcg.org/programmes/us/us_life. html. *Toolbox* also discusses the abortion issue and environmental ethics at length. For a general next step into environmental ethics, see my collection *An Invitation to Environmental Philosophy* (Oxford University Press, 1999), including its extensive annotated bibliography, "Going On."

NOTES FOR TEACHERS

This book is primarily intended as a supplementary text for a university- or secondary-level ethics course. It does not presuppose any particular approach to ethics or meta-ethics. It is also compatible with a wide variety of main texts. In any course where students are invited to address real, practical ethical issues, creative problem solving is a relevant—in fact, absolutely vital— skill.

This book is also intended to be self-explanatory. In class, head straight into practice. Each chapter's "For Practice" section gives you a good start. Students enjoy this kind of work; it gives practical results that can make a real difference; and anyway, in the end, there is just no other way to develop the skills. Learning to think creatively is much more like learning to play piano, say, than studying music theory. Reading or lecturing about it can only be prelude.

Use the warm-ups and the wilder exercises, too. Even though they are less immediately practical, they help limber up the mind for the more serious work and can introduce a note of playfulness that ethics sorely needs as well.

Teachers unfamiliar with this material should take a bit of care with their own initial attitudes. Creative thinking is not so familiar in ethics and can readily be undercut from our side as well: by not giving the methods enough time to work (especially the more improbable ones, like exotic association), by moving too fast to "edit" or tone down students' initial ideas once they do come up with them, or by unintentionally privileging traditional formulations of problems. Teaching this material works best when teachers can wholeheartedly model the very attitudes that they are trying to teach. Give students a lot of space and a lot of provocation (they sometimes need to be nudged into *really using* some of these methods). And don't let them stop with ideas that are only a little out of the box. Look at their ideas midstream, but then challenge them to take their ideas to another level of creativity. Use brainstorming groups, say, and remix the groups periodically. The sky is the limit here. We fail more often not by asking too much but by expecting too little.

Along these lines, I want to add a bit more about my treatment of the Heinz dilemma in Chapter 1, as this goes to the very heart of how this book relates to ethics as traditionally conceived. Ethical philosophers typically encounter the Kohlberg dilemmas as illustrations of the divergences and conflicts between major ethical theories, especially between utilitarian and deontological theories. And, of course, if that is your interest in the dilemmas, you can alter them in various ways to close off the possibility of other alternatives. I have even seen ethics textbooks in which students aren't considered to have understood the issue until they identify "the" dilemma that is supposed to lie at the root of it.

The problem, of course, is that this essentially makes ethical problems dilemmas by fiat. It simply *builds in* the assumption that dilemmas are, after all, what we typically face. But are they? How can we know without creatively seeking alternatives? This requires different attitudes from the start, as I have tried to show; and I hope it is also evident from this book that many alleged dilemmas actually can be resolved or at least constructively reframed. The supposed dilemma between utilitarianism and deontological ethics itself has come in for some question, even theoretically; but even if these theories do conflict, one could construe their conflict as another practical creative challenge—to so design social institutions that these different sets of values seldom or only harmlessly conflict in practice. That an entire approach to ethics should instead be built around the supposedly fundamental conflict is not the only possible response. Surely, at the very least, such an approach is not entitled to claim with no further ado that it alone constitutes "ethics" itself.

Sometimes my students try to cook up dilemmas that really do allow no other options. That's a useful discussion too, but for the most part, it is worth trying to set up the dynamics in the opposite direction. See if they can cook up situations that *look* like complete traps but really have dramatic new options. This is the point, in part, of the scriptwriter challenge in exercise 2 for Chapter 4. I believe that it makes much more practical sense to encourage students (and ourselves!) to approach ethical problems first in this more open-ended way and only then let ourselves be driven, if need be, into more restrictive views. Start with restrictive views, contrariwise, and we're unlikely to ever go anywhere at all.

Students should be asked to read through all of the "For Practice" sections, even if you do not assign all of them for actual practice—there are substantive ideas and useful suggestions there in any case.

The "For Practice" section of Chapter 6 ends the book by challenging students to take their results back out into the world and change some things. This is not so easy or so familiar either, but it can also be transformative not just of the world (we hope) but of individual students and indeed of the class as a whole. Consider closing the class, or this portion of it, with some such project. I would be honored to hear of these, as well as any other suggestions you might have for improving this book.